Dried Flowers

A COMPLETE GUIDE

Lindy Bird

GUILD OF MASTER CRAFTSMAN PUBLICATIONS

First published 2003 by
Guild of Master Craftsman Publications Ltd,
166 High Street, Lewes,
East Sussex, BN7 1XN

Photographs by Anthony Bailey except pages 19-20,105-107 © Juliette Wade;
pages 20, 22, 37, 93, 96–97, 99 © Sally Phipps Hornby;
pages 20–21, 36, 91, 102, 104 © Jeremy Bird;
page 108 © David Bird;
page 2 © The Bridgeman Art Library;
pages 79, 81, 109 © *Farmers' Weekly*
Illustrations by John Yates

ISBN 1 86108 365 3

Publisher: Paul Richardson
Art Director: Ian Smith
Production Manager: Matt Weyland
Managing Editor: April McCroskie
Editor: Clare Miller

Cover and book design by Phil and Traci Morash at Fineline Studios
Cover photograph by Anthony Bailey

Typeface: Hiroshige

Colour origination by Universal Graphics (Singapore)

Printed and bound in Hong Kong by CT Printing Ltd

Dried Flowers

A Complete Guide

Dedication

This book is dedicated to David, with my love and thanks for his help and support over this, and many other projects. Also to the memory of Francis Short, without whose help and expertise our flower growing would never have been so successful.

Contents

Introduction

*W*ho, I wonder, ever thought of drying flowers? Looked at rationally, it seems an extraordinary thing to do – perhaps it was a progression from the practice of drying herbs to cure illness. It seems that the reasons must be lost in the mists of time, but however it came about, the use of flowers for decoration has been referred to throughout history.

Lotus flowers are often depicted on wall decorations in the tombs of ancient Egypt as were floral garlands and tributes to the dead. Bouquets, bowers and vases of flowers appear in many Old Master paintings. One of the first references to drying flowers comes from the great plant collector John Tradescant, who sent back specimens for King Charles I from his travels in 1618–1620, when he recorded, 'Flower laid betwin paper leaves in a book, dried to be sent home'. This is an early example of flower pressing, which was to prove a useful tool for the identification of different species.

At the same time, around the early 1600s, references to the drying of flowers in sand start to appear. Perhaps interest then waned, as little is written on the subject until the Victorians discovered the extraordinary lasting qualities of some newly introduced species – the so-called 'immortelles'. *Helichrysum*, statice (*Limonium*) and *Helipterum acroclinium* really came into their own at that time together with great plumes of pampas grass and Chinese lanterns, and it seems there

was barely a house in the land from cottage to manor without a dried decoration of some sort.

Over recent years flower drying has once again become popular, but this has its downside. In order to cash in on the great boom, flowers are mass produced and kiln dried, then crammed into boxes to be shipped around the world. There is a considerable difference in quality between these brittle and sometimes crushed offerings, often sold in bunches or unnatural-looking arrangements, and those that have been cut fresh from a garden, dried with care and used around the house during winter as a reminder of warmer days.

My fascination with the subject began after many years of putting my heart and soul into creating fresh flower arrangements that then withered and died a few days later. Breughel and other Dutch artists were a great inspiration as many of their paintings include flowers from every season. With this in mind, it became my goal to find a way of extending the life of flowers and retaining their colour and shape, in order to create natural-looking arrangements that spanned the seasons.

Flowers in a Terracotta Vase (1736) Jan van Huysum

We are lucky in having a large garden which, at the start of my experiments, already contained many of the flowers and foliage I had visualized using. Gradually, over a period of nearly 20 years, I added different types until I had accumulated a vast collection with which to try out various drying techniques. Some I discarded as being either unsuccessful or uninteresting, and it is only those that I have found to be the most effective for drying that have been included in this book.

Due to my insistence on always using flowers and foliage in their natural colours, I have sometimes rather disparagingly been called a purist; as other designers used dried flowers that were spray-painted or dyed, often in so-called 'designer colours'. To my mind this is a nonsense, as the natural colours that can be achieved by careful drying are every bit as brilliant and far more attractive than the often garish alternatives. While these flowers and their colours will not last for ever, I have often seen displays five, or even as long as ten years after I made them, and although they have mellowed, there is still a certain amount of colour in them and that charm which belongs exclusively to dried flowers. Anybody who wants a flower display to last forever should use silk flowers as there are some on the market which are totally lifelike, but they should be looked upon as a substitute for fresh flowers not, as in the case of dried flowers, decorative items in their own right.

Some of the floristry and growing methods described in this book may be considered unorthodox, but experience has taught me to break established rules sometimes, and the methods I have included all work for me.

My hope is that readers will be inspired either to make a garden or to add to an existing one by growing flowers and foliage that can be enjoyed all year round, both inside the house and out.

A watercolour of Malt House Flower Farm by John Silk

METHODS OF

Preserving
Flowers

METHODS OF
Preserving Flowers

*I*n this chapter I outline the various methods for preserving flowers. The first is really a traditional method, while some of the others are more modern. But drying of some description is an ancient method for preserving flowers and will no doubt continue into the future.

Air drying

This is the age-old method of preserving flowers by hanging bunches in a dry area where there is a good circulation of air. Most attics, outbuildings, sheds or garages are suitable as long as the flowers are brought into the house once they are quite dry, before they can be damaged by moist autumn air.

Depending upon the type of flowers to be dried, bunches are normally made of a size which your hand can comfortably fit around. They can be secured using twine which is doubled to form a loop, then the two ends pulled through the loop around the bunch. This will tighten as the flowers dry and prevent them falling out. But the best method is to use rubber bands. Holding the bunch in one hand, hook the band over three or four stems with your other hand (Fig 1.1), wrap it round the bunch once or twice, then loop the band over

Fig 1.1 Holding a 'twist tie' in place, slip a rubber band over several stems in the bunch

Fig 1.2 Wrapping the band around the bunch

several more stems (Fig 1.2). I like to attach these bunches to the wire coat hangers we all collect from dry cleaners, either tying them in the case of twine, or using a 'twist tie' when rubber bands are used. This makes good use of space as each hanger will hold four or five bunches (Fig 1.3). If the beam or pole where they are to be hung is out of reach, this can easily be overcome by screwing a cup hook into the end of a bamboo cane and using it to hoist up the hangers.

Some flowers do not lend themselves to being bunched in this manner, delphiniums for instance are better dried by hanging individually. This can be done simply by forming a short piece of florists' wire into a small 's' hook (Fig 1.4), pushing one end into the stem and hooking the other over the hanger bar.

Air drying with additional heat

This is merely a way of speeding up the drying process and thereby improving the colour of the resulting dried flowers. Larkspur is one type of flower that benefits from this treatment and others can be found in the directory at the end of this book. For most people, an airing cupboard is quite adequate for the purpose, otherwise hanging the bunches in a cupboard with an electric dehumidifier will do the job quickly and efficiently. If the cupboard is small, the door should be left slightly open to allow circulation of air.

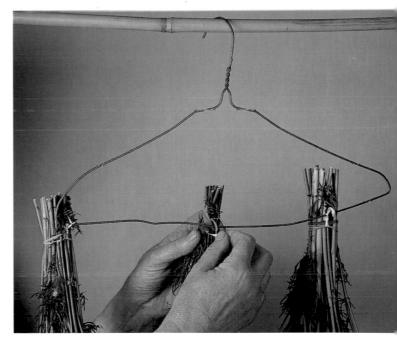

Fig 1.3 Attaching the bunch to a wire hanger with the 'twist tie'

Fig 1.4 Pushing a wire 's' hook through a delphinium stem prior to hanging it over a hanger

Fig 1.5 Peony and rose heads pushed firmly into a layer of silica gel

Fig 1.6 Pouring silica gel over the flowers

Desiccant preserving

The practice of burying plant material in a silica substance to draw out the moisture is an ancient one. In earlier times, dry sand was used, as indeed it still can be. But we now have a modern equivalent in the form of a chemically produced silica gel. The advantage of using this, as opposed to sand, is that it acts more quickly and leaves the flowers barely altered from their fresh state. Silica gel is quite expensive to buy initially, but as it can be dried and reused indefinitely, it is well worth the initial investment.

To preserve flowers by this method, you will need a plastic box with a tight-fitting lid. Pour in about 3cm (1in) of silica gel to make a bed on which to lay or stand the flowers, push the base of the flowers firmly into the desiccant keeping them upright if possible (Fig 1.5). Using a jug or a spoon fill the area around the flower heads with the crystals first, then from above, cover the petals completely until all the flowers are buried (Figs 1.6 and 1.7).

Put on the lid and leave the box in a warm place for four to seven days. Some flowers will be completely dry in this time, others will need a little longer. It is impossible to give an exact timing for any particular flower as so much depends on the moisture content at the time of picking. As a general rule, fleshy flowers such as peonies take longer than those like hellebores, which in their fresh state feel fairly dry to the touch. To test for dryness, tip the box to reveal the top of a flower. Feel the petals and if they are dry and papery all the flowers are likely to be ready, otherwise leave them for a few more days. These timings are the minimum that flowers will take to dry, they will come to no harm if they are left in the silica gel for longer. I would, however, advise against leaving them for longer than a month as any remaining moisture continues to be removed and this will result in some loss of colour.

The consistency of silica gel is an important factor in this type of preserving; it must be of the correct grade for flower drying which is roughly the same as granulated sugar. Probably the best way to get hold of it would be to ask a local florist to buy some for you from a wholesaler. I generally advise people to buy 2kg (4lb), as an average ice cream box will hold approximately 1kg (2lb), and you will then have enough to dry out for further use at the same time as preserving your flowers. If the silica gel is supplied with a humidity indicator card this will change colour from blue to pink when it has absorbed enough moisture and needs drying – simply a matter of pouring it into a roasting tin then into the oven set to 100°C (200°F) for three hours. The drying can also be done in a microwave. Use an uncovered microwave-proof dish, and with the setting on full power, dry no more than about 500g (1lb) at a time for approximately eight minutes, stirring once or twice during the process. Always allow the silica gel to cool completely before using it for flower drying. Even without an indicator card you will soon learn how to tell when the crystals need drying as you will find it takes an increasingly long time to draw out the moisture from flowers.

Fig 1.7 The flowers almost buried in silica gel

An important point about silica gel is to store it at all times in a sealed plastic container. Cardboard and tin boxes are not really suitable as they allow it to absorb a certain amount of moisture from the atmosphere and this reduces its efficiency.

There are various ways to make the crystals go further. One useful tip is to fill the bottom of your container with 3cm (1in) florists' foam and push the flower heads into that before filling around them with crystals. Another is to mix the silica gel with an equal quantity of well-dried silver sand or bird sand, though this will probably lengthen the drying time. Borax is sometimes recommended as a drying medium, but I have never had success with it. Other alternatives are cat litter and washing powder. None of these works as well as pure silica gel.

After drying in a desiccant, it is essential to finish the process in a warm or dehumidified place

Fig 1.8 Dried peony and zinnia heads ready for storage

in order that the flower calyx and stem dry out completely, otherwise moisture from these will seep up into the petals which results in the colour fading. Egg boxes are useful for the final drying and storage of flowers like roses. For peonies and other larger flowers, the shaped containers within wooden trays that are used to transport fruit, are excellent for storage purposes (Fig 1.8).

Microwave drying

Flowers are generally dried by this method buried in silica gel in exactly the same way as has already been described. The only difference being that it is better to use an oven-proof dish or other microwaveable container, covered with either a lid or clingfilm. It is best to dry only one or two flowers at a time, and leave them in the silica gel until it is cold. Depending upon the type of oven, two to three minutes on full power is usually long enough, though after testing the tip of a petal for dryness, you may find that the flowers need a minute or two more. The microwave can be useful if material is needed in a hurry, but the results are not as good, nor as long lasting, as 'normal' silica gel drying.

A microwave oven can also be useful for the speedy drying of leaves if different shades and textures are needed for some specific purpose. They should be layered between sheets of paper towel, then held down by a container filled with enough sand to hold them flat.

Some flowers can be dried in a microwave by simply laying them on a paper towel or a perforated plastic rack. I sometimes find, to my delight, that flowers can have two incarnations. Zinnias and rudbeckia can be used in fresh flower arrangements until they start to look a bit 'past it', and then dried off in the microwave for two to three minutes. They will be reduced in size, but

the colours remain superb, making them useful additions for later arrangements. There may be many more flowers that respond to drying in this way, so it is well worth experimenting with different types.

Drying and pressing foliage

Some types of foliage dry beautifully and keep their green colour for a long time if sprigs and sprays are simply laid flat in a warm place (Fig 1.9). Sweet gum (*Eucalyptus*) is undoubtedly the best, followed by box, myrtle and *Pittosporum*. Foliage of the 'bottle brush' shrub (*Callistemon*) is another useful one, but this is better dried by hanging in small bunches.

Fig 1.9 *Pittosporum*, myrtle and sweet gum leaves that have been dried by laying flat in a warm place

Fig 1.10 Lay ferns on a newspaper ready for pressing

Fig 1.11 Place a board on top of the ferns once they are covered with newspaper

Some leaves need to be pressed for the best results, though preparing them for use is a bit of a chore, as each one needs to be individually wired. The simplest way to do this is to use a glue gun to attach a florists' wire to the back. Provided the wire is not too thick, adhesive tape will also work well. Almost any type of leaf can be treated in this way. Particularly nice are the autumn tints of maples (*Acer*), and virginia creeper (*Parthenocissus*); just one or two of these leaves will add a richness of colour to arrangements.

Green ferns are one of the most spectacular of all pressed leaves, and they can be used both for outlining and throughout large dried displays. They take up rather a lot of space in a press, but are definitely worth the effort.

There is no need to invest in an expensive flower press. A makeshift one is easy to assemble, and on the whole more successful, as the pressure is not so great as with the standard type that is screwed down. All the leaves need is to be held flat as they dry. Use a large piece of wooden board as a base, big enough to accommodate an opened sheet of newspaper (Fig 1.10). Lay a few newspaper sheets on it, followed by your chosen leaves, then another layer of paper, and so on. It can then be topped with another board, roughly the same size as the first (Fig 1.11), and then pushed out of the way under a bed or sofa. You can add to it at any time, simply by piling on more layers of paper and leaves. Provided the 'press' is kept in a reasonably warm and dry place, the leaves should be dry enough to use in four to six weeks, though they will come to no harm if they are left in it for a longer period.

A quick alternative is to press leaves with a warm iron, between two sheets of kitchen towel, until they feel quite dry to the touch. Once dried in this way, they will need to be stored under a book, or something similar, to keep them flat until they are used.

Skeletonizing leaves

The best skeletonized materials are those which occur naturally over a long period. It is often a matter of keeping a sharp lookout for seed-heads and leaves that the elements have stripped entirely of their outer skin, leaving an exquisite lace-like pattern (Fig 1.12). They are shown to their best advantage when used as part of a dried flower picture on a dark background. Alternatively, bunches of the leaves can be used to create a misty and romantic effect in certain arrangements.

The process can be achieved artificially but is a rather smelly business as it involves soaking tough evergreen leaves in a bucket of rainwater which must not be changed. After several weeks, the outer skins can be gently rubbed away leaving just the 'skeleton'. The best leaves to use are laurel, magnolia, ivy and camellia.

Glycerine preserving

The nice thing about foliage preserved in glycerine is that it is totally different from dried leaves, and so a mixture of the two adds depth and interest to dried flower arrangements.

It is important to remember that most foliage for preserving in this way must be mature and, in the case of deciduous leaves such as beech, not left too late. Once they begin to change colour in autumn, they are not able to absorb enough glycerine, but even when picked green in late summer, beech leaves will turn rust-coloured after treatment. Sprays of oak leaves, picked from young trees, preserve best in early summer. There are numerous types of evergreen foliage that respond well to this preservation process: bay, laurel, camellia and *Photinia* to mention a few, though these will sometimes take months to absorb the liquid. Rosehips and some types of berries, such as *Cotoneaster multiflorus*, together with their leaves, can also be successfully treated in autumn.

The process is very simple: use one part glycerine to two parts of water, boil them together and then allow to cool. Put the mixture in a jar and stand this inside a bucket which will prevent the jar falling over if long sprays of leaves are used (Fig 1.13). Cut the stems at an angle and simply stand them in the mixture. There is no need for

Fig 1.12 Chinese lanterns that have been skeletonized naturally by the weather, and ivy and camellia leaves where this has been artificially achieved by soaking in rainwater

splitting or hammering the stems. It is impossible to give exact timings for each type of foliage, as it depends upon the time of year and the speed with which the glycerine is absorbed, but for most plant material three weeks is a good average time, after which the leaves should be regularly inspected. When they have absorbed enough of the mixture, a faint glimmer can be seen on the backs of the leaves. At this point they should be removed from the solution and laid flat in a dry place. It is important not to be tempted to bunch and hang them out of the way as this causes the glycerine to seep further into the leaves, causing mildew. If the leaves are stored in a damp place once they are preserved, it is possible that some mildew will develop anyway. This can easily be wiped off with a damp cloth without doing any damage. The mixed glycerine solution can be used

can be a nuisance if there is a bad infestation where silica gel dried flowers are stored. The female moth likes to search out secluded places in which to lay her eggs, and a favourite spot is within the petals of dried roses and peonies. The problem with this is that no sign will be seen until the grub has hatched and eaten its way out of the flower; often after it has been used in an arrangement. The flower will suddenly fall apart leaving nothing but a few petals, some cobweb-like strands and moth droppings!

Prevention is difficult unless specialist sprays are used on all affected surfaces such as walls and shelves during mid-summer, when the moths are at their most active. These kill any insect that lands on the treated surfaces. Such sprays are not really suitable for use in a domestic environment, so the best advice is to be vigilant, and if any moths are seen, a normal fly spray should be used in the area immediately, not just once, but on a regular basis. Moth balls among the stored flowers are helpful and fly papers can be used to trap any flying moths, with luck before they have laid their eggs.

Mildew can occur all too easily if preserved material is stored in an area that is not completely dry. In temperate climates this means using either some background heat or a dehumidifier.

These warnings should not put anybody off this fascinating hobby, and all these problems can easily be prevented by using your harvested flowers just as soon as the last ones are dry, so that they may be brought into the house and enjoyed throughout the whole winter.

repeatedly but it is a good idea to boil it between uses. If, after some time, it becomes very thick, add a little more water when boiling, and then strain the mixture through butter muslin. In this way, you can keep it going almost indefinitely.

Storage

Mice, moths and mildew. These are the three main enemies of a dried flower store. The first because they eat anything edible, which means seed-heads such as poppies, any types of grasses, and cereals such as wheat and oats.

Consequently, anywhere mice are likely to be a problem vulnerable dried material needs to be either stored in mouse-proof boxes, such as metal trunks, or hung well out of reach. Clothes moths

Fig 1.14 Roses and peonies drying in silica gel

GROWING
Flowers for
Drying

GROWING
Flowers for Drying

*B*efore embarking on growing flowers
specifically for drying, it is useful to know which
are the most suitable and the best propagation
methods for the different types.

Choosing seeds

Most gardeners agree that one of winter's great
pleasures is planning for the coming season. Seed
catalogues allow the imagination to run wild with
plans for new plants and fantastic colour schemes.
An added dimension is the inclusion of dual-purpose
plants that fill the borders with their brilliant summer
colour and can then be dried for use over the
following winter; thus making a garden that covers
all seasons, both inside the house and out.

Where the plants are to be grown is the first
consideration. In most gardens with mixed
borders there will be space for some annuals,
though in larger gardens it may be possible to use
a plot that is devoted purely to flowers for cutting.
However, it seems a pity not to grow such
abundant and colourful flowers where they can
be seen; after all, not every flower will be ready
for picking at the same moment.

The easiest flowers to grow are undoubtedly
those which are straw textured, so no garden
should be without some strawflowers (*Helichrysum
brachteatum*), statice (*Limonium*) and pink pokers
(*Psylliostachys suworowii*). These three will provide
some really strong colours (Fig 2.1). Add to these
some of the dainty pink and white daisies listed as
Helipterum or *Rhodanthe* (Fig 2.2). I prefer the
latter as their heads remain upright when dry.

Fig 2.1 Harvesting flowers, including pink pokers,
gypsophila and larkspur, at the farm

Fig 2.2 Harvested *Rhodanthe* ready for bunching

Fig 2.3 An array of magnificent larkspur flowers

given to me by a professional larkspur grower: ten days after autumn sowing (which is usually the time it takes for weed seeds to germinate) spray the entire area with half-strength Weedol or a similar weedkiller containing diquat and paraquat. This will eradicate most weeds, and as the larkspur takes longer to germinate it will then be able to grow in a weed-free bed.

Next must come a few packets of larkspur, the real queen of dried flowers (Fig 2.3). These seeds should always be sown where they are to flower, and give the best results of all when sown during the first two weeks of September. The warmth of the soil at that time of year encourages them to germinate fast and emerge before the weeds, which otherwise engulf spring-sown plants. Overwintering is no problem and they should have towering flower spikes by the following July. A useful tip was

Other seeds that are best sown in autumn are annual poppies, and as only the seed-heads are used for drying, the flowers make a good splash of summer colour over a long period (Fig 2.4). Leave a few seed-heads to mature and they will self-seed and continue to produce more plants each year. *Nigella* ('Love-in-a-mist') is another good self-seeder which does best when autumn sown. The beauty of this plant is that you can first enjoy the pink and blue flowers set against their green haze, and then use the seed-heads for later drying.

Fig 2.4 Annual poppies

Fig 2.5 Red amaranthus

Spring sowings of all these seeds can be made, but the plants will not be as large and they will flower later. Sometimes, in a flower bed, it is a good compromise to have half autumn- and half spring-sown annuals to give a good succession during the entire summer.

All these pastel and brightly coloured plants will need some contrast to set them off, so my next choice would be red and green amaranthus ('Pigmy Torch' and 'Tom Thumb') (Fig 2.5). These are simple to grow, and once you have them, they too will freely cast their seed around the garden (often growing in the most unsuitable places). Alternatively, once the spikes are dry you can rub some seeds off and keep them for sowing the following spring.

Another useful and showy red plant is *Atriplex hortensis* ('Red Orach') which will grow to about 1.2m (4ft). The seed-covered spikes dry well and the young leaves can also be eaten in salads.

Fig 2.6 *Carthamus tinctorius*

Sapphire-blue cornflower plants reliably reappear each year, and a few clumps dotted throughout the border create dramatic contrasts, particularly when sown next to drifts of *Carthamus tinctorius* (Fig 2.6). These are bright green, many-branched, thistle-like plants with brilliant orange, yellow or cream tufts on top of their heads. Another good yellow flower is *Lonas inodora* which resembles a miniature achillea. *Nicandra*, the 'Shoo Fly Plant', with its blue flowers and green lanterns should not be forgotten and, once established, it too will always reappear the following year.

Amongst all this colour, some white flowers are usually called for, and from the drying point of view, three of the best are the starry flowered ammobium with pure white papery petals; the florist's favourite, gypsophila, and a little 'everlasting' with the long-winded name *Xeranthemum*. This is often sold in

Fig 2.7 Zinnias ready to be picked for drying

mixed packets which will include light and dark pink colours as well as white.

To complete the list of useful annuals, I would not be without *Moluccella* (the green 'Bells of Ireland'), African marigolds, large-flowered double zinnias and a good mixture of *Rudbeckia* (Fig 2.7).

A packet or two of mixed grasses can provide useful material for the dried flower store though I usually grow these in a corner on their own rather than in the flower bed – it can sometimes be difficult to distinguish them from weeds.

For those with a little patience, perennials, too, can easily be raised from seed. In most cases they will not flower until the following year, but it is an inexpensive and satisfying way of making a garden.

With drying in mind, I would first go for the largest clump of true blue delphiniums possible, followed by masses of *Achillea* in yellow, white and the pretty salmon and red mixtures.

White anaphalis, *Alchemilla mollis* and carline thistles all look good at the front of a border and the flowers dry like a dream, whilst clumps of acanthus are useful at the back.

Steely blue *Eryngium* and *Echinops* are both indispensable for the flower dryer, and their sculptural shapes, together with some enormous cardoon plants, look magnificent in a border.

Well known amongst most flower dryers is the white *Statice dumosa*. Contrary to belief, this is really quite easy to grow, and being a perennial type of statice, is trouble free once it is established in the garden and can be harvested every year. The disadvantage is that it is not an attractive plant. The top-heavy, flower-laden sprays rise awkwardly above small rosettes of green leaves and do little to enhance a flower border. They are best grown in a corner on their own, where the flowers can be harvested, and then the plants forgotten until the following summer.

Some marjoram and chives are well worth growing as the flowers are not only useful 'fillers' for dried arrangements but the leaves are invaluable in cooking.

The last in this list of perennials, I mention with hesitation. Chinese lanterns are invaluable for dried flower decoration, but a real nuisance in a flower bed. Once established, they take over the entire area, and are almost impossible to eradicate as they can spread from a minute scrap of root. They make a lovely display in late summer and autumn, but are best given their own space, well away from other plants.

Many bulbs and plants with tuberous roots can also be raised from seed; though they can take several years to produce flowers it is an inexpensive way of increasing their number. Bulb seeds should always be sown in pots, as they need a good depth of compost in which to develop. They should be left undisturbed for about two years, after which time fair sized bulbs should have developed, which can then be planted outside. Dahlias, on the other hand, will flower the same year they are sown and no flower dryer's garden should be without plenty of the pom-pom and ball types, which retain both shape and colour when dried in silica gel. Small tubers develop over the summer and can be lifted in autumn, then replanted the following spring. Once well established, the tubers may be able to remain in the ground in mild areas during winter.

Sowing seeds under glass

Most seeds that benefit from being started in an unheated greenhouse or polytunnel, should be sown during early spring, in order to get as long a season as possible. Of course, in a heated greenhouse they can be started even earlier, but then there can be a problem with plants becoming ever larger, and outgrowing their seed trays should outside planting be delayed by a wet spring.

When reusing seed trays and pots, it is important to remember that they must always be cleaned thoroughly, to prevent the spread of disease. The best way is to wash them well in a solution of any good garden disinfectant, such as Jeyes Fluid.

Those without a greenhouse, who would like their plants to get an early start, can easily make a simple cold frame using a fairly thick clear plastic, and wire of the type used for fencing. Cut a piece of plastic 100cm (39in) by 79cm (31in) and three pieces of wire 135cm (53in) long. Turn in about 2.5cm (1in) on each of the shorter sides and stick them down with tough adhesive tape (such as Duck Tape). Using the same tape, stick a narrow strip of plastic across the centre. There are now three channels through which the wire can be threaded. When the ends of the wire are pushed into the ground the plastic will form a useful small polytunnel (Fig 2.8). Extra pieces of plastic can be taped over each end to be let down and held in place with stones on cold nights. A little polytunnel like this will hold around five standard size seed trays.

Fig 2.8 The seedbed covered with a makeshift cold frame

Fig 2.9 The board used to mark sowing holes

In order to save valuable time pricking out young plants, and the trauma it causes them, I like to carefully space the seeds when I am sowing. This sounds difficult and painstaking, but is actually quite easy. My method is to cut a piece of board, roughly the same size as the top of a seed tray, and mark one side into squares approximately 5cm (2in) apart. Using these squares as a guide, tap in round-headed upholstery nails leaving about 1cm (½in) protruding (Fig 2.9). Attach a handle to the other side of the board (Fig 2.10). You then have a perfect marker, which makes 28 small indentations in the compost-filled seed tray. To make it easier to see the marks, scatter silver sand over the compost before sowing. A sand-filled screw-top jar with holes punched in the lid is useful for this purpose (Fig 2.11).

Fig 2.10 Pressing the board firmly on to the compost

Most people have their own preference of ways to sow. I like to use a multi-purpose compost mixed with silver sand (two parts compost to one of sand). Fill the seed trays to within 1.5cm (½in) from the top, then water the compost thoroughly; once the compost is well soaked, spray the surface lightly with a well-diluted solution of ammonium carbonate copper sulphate, such as Cheshunt Compound. This will prevent the seedlings from contracting a fungal disease called 'damping off', which causes them to keel over and die soon after

Fig 2.11 Shaking sand over the compost in order to make the sowing holes more visible

Fig 2.12 Sowing seeds using tweezers

Fig 2.13 Sieving compost thinly over the sown seeds

Fig 2.14 Covering the seed tray with clingfilm

Fig 2.15 Placing newspaper over the top

emerging. (These compounds should be available in most good garden centres.)

Mark the surface of the compost as described, and sow each seed separately, using a pair of tweezers (Fig 2.12). Finally, sift some more compost, or vermiculite, over the whole tray to lightly cover the seeds (Fig 2.13); then place a piece of glass or tightly stretched clingfilm over the top (Fig 2.14), and cover that with a sheet of newspaper (Fig 2.15). It is unlikely that every single seed will germinate, so due to the fact that they are sparingly sown, it is best to take the precaution of sowing an extra tray or two.

Germination can be surprisingly quick and after about a week the trays should be inspected on a daily basis. As soon as the first shoots are seen take off the newspaper then, when the tiny seedlings reach the glass or clingfilm, remove that too. Keep the seed trays lightly watered as necessary, using water from the mains rather than collected rain water, which can contain bacteria harmful to small plants. Sometimes mice can be a problem, they burrow into the compost presumably searching for seeds, so if there is any danger of this, cover the trays with a net or small-mesh wire netting. I always scatter slug pellets all round the area, as one slug can devour a whole tray of seedlings in a night.

All the perennials I have mentioned are best started under glass. The following annuals are those that benefit from an early start: strawflower (*Helichrysum brachteatum*), statice (*Limonium*), pink pokers, *Ammobium*, *Xeranthemum*, African marigolds, zinnias and *Rudbeckia*.

Moluccella seems to do best if sown in a pot or seed tray during autumn, then left uncovered in a frost-free place inside a black plastic sack until germination can be seen in spring. Most of these seeds can be sown directly outside, but then their flowering season will be short.

Fig 2.16 Sowing seed thinly in the drill

Fig 2.17 Firming down the soil with a rake

Fig 2.18 A seed bed protected by twigs

Outdoor sowing

It is impossible to give an exact time when outdoor sowing can be carried out as it is dependent on weather. I always used to fret if wet weather delayed my sowing after early spring, but I have now come to the conclusion that it is perfectly possible to leave it until close to the onset of summer. This can be an advantage, as by then the soil has warmed and this encourages the seeds to germinate rapidly. Also the first crop of weeds can be removed, giving the tiny seedlings more space when they first emerge.

If flowers are to be grown in an area specifically for cutting, the ground should first be dug over or rotavated, then raked to a fine tilth. There is no need to rake the entire area, just mark where each row will be and rake that strip. If several rows of one variety are to be grown, they can generally be sown in two to four shallow furrows, known as 'drills'. Make these with the corner of a hoe, approximately 20cm (8in) apart, then leave around 70cm (28in) before making the next set of drills. Use a line to keep the rows reasonably straight. Once the seed is sown (Fig 2.16), lightly cover the drill with soil, then firm it well using the back of a rake or a shovel (Fig 2.17).

Sowing in a mixed flower bed is a different matter. First the soil must be prepared as described, then, having decided where each variety will be grown, mark the shape in which you want your clump by trickling sand around the outline. Using a stick, make shallow seed drills within this shape, either in straight lines or curves, so that it will be easy to distinguish flowers from weeds as they grow. Sow the seed thinly in the drills, then cover with soil and flatten it as described. Most seedlings will need a certain amount of thinning once they emerge. Small plants can be left to grow relatively close together, but larger ones, annual poppies in particular, need to be ruthlessly thinned to approximately 24cm (10in) apart, or the plants will remain very small, flower quickly and then fade, leaving only tiny seed-heads for drying.

Fig 2.19
Planting out strawflower seedlings

Large plants will give a much longer flowering season and produce giant seed-heads.

From now on, birds, weeds and slugs will be the main problems to look out for. There are few things more annoying than seeing a pigeon scratching at your newly sown bed, gobbling seeds as it goes. Twigs spread over the top act as a good deterrent (Fig 2.18), or for a larger area, some 'humming lines' can be stretched over the top between bamboo canes. This is strong, thin plastic tape (available in garden centres) that is supposed to make a sound almost inaudible to the human ear, but either irritating or frightening to birds.

Weeding is a must, until the plants have grown to a reasonable size, otherwise the competition between prolific weeds and tiny seedlings is too great. When the seeds are sown in rows, hoeing can be the answer, but in flower beds it usually has to be done by hand.

Precautions should always be taken against slugs eating the tiny seedlings just as they emerge. Either slug pellets or the more environmentally friendly types of slug destroyer can be scattered around. Alternatively, surround the plants with crushed egg shells and sink beer-filled yoghurt pots at intervals throughout the area. The slugs will go out of their way to avoid scratching their tummies and instead will drown in glorious oblivion.

Planting out

As the weather gets warmer, the plant trays should be left outside for a while, so that the seedlings can be hardened off. Around two months after sowing, they will be ready for planting outside in their summer positions (Fig 2.19). By this time they should have good roots and the disturbance of transplanting will be minimal. Most of the annuals mentioned can be planted about 15cm (6in) apart, and the colours will make more impact if all the different types are kept together in large groups.

Taking cuttings and plant propagation

Television programmes and magazines are constantly encouraging us to grow this or that plant in our gardens, but they often fail to mention the cost. Luckily, many plants that can be used for drying can also easily be augmented by taking cuttings. There are several aromatic ones that root readily. Curry plant, lavender, myrtle and rosemary are some of the easiest; followed by silver foliage plants such as *Ballota*, *Phlomis* and *Santolina*. Roses, hydrangeas and box are not quite so easy, but as a rule, one or two out of a pot-full will take root.

Fig 2.20
Trimming the 'heel' of a lavender cutting

Fig 2.21
Dipping the cutting into hormone rooting powder

bed consists of a wooden frame lined with plastic, the whole thing is then filled with sand, which is kept damp at all times. Of course it does not have to be on a large scale; any form of plastic container, from a children's sandpit to a polystyrene box of the type used by fishmongers to transport fish, will do just as well. Without a greenhouse or polytunnel, a cold frame would do the job or, failing that, a sheltered corner of the garden. It is important to take a fair number of cuttings each time as some will invariably fail to root. As a rule, I put in about ten and expect half to grow.

The time taken to root can be anything from a few weeks to a few months. Never be tempted to remove any cuttings that are still showing signs of life, even after as long as six or nine months; your patience may eventually be rewarded!

Once the cuttings have rooted and appear to be growing healthily, it is best to leave them in their original pot until the roots can be seen coming through the bottom. They will do this fairly rapidly as they seek moisture in the damp sand. Now is the time to transplant each one into individual pots containing compost mixed with a little bonemeal. This will help the roots to develop and allow them room to grow. If they have been rooted under glass, leave them there for a few weeks to recover from the shock, then in spring, move them outside to an outdoor sand bed, or sink the pots into the soil to ensure they do not dry out. By the following autumn, you should have any number of healthy plants to add to your garden.

Division is one of the simplest ways to increase existing plants. Most herbaceous perennials can simply be split by cutting off portions with a knife or spade, or forcing them apart with two forks. The latter can be tricky to achieve so I usually opt for the knife method, which I find to be accurate and infallible.

Some plants will grow easily from a piece pulled off the parent. *Stachys byzantina* and most types of *Persicaria* respond well to this method, as do the majority of plants with a similar creeping habit. Some others do well from a side shoot with

My method of taking cuttings is always the same. During late summer and early autumn I select suitable shoots on the plant or shrub. These are generally about 15–20cm (6–8in) long and, where possible, new growth that has not flowered. I pull them from the main stem ensuring that they have a tiny portion of that stem (or 'heel') attached (Fig 2.20). This is then trimmed to get rid of the ragged edge. Using a mixture (about half and half) of multi-purpose compost and sharp sand filled into flowerpots, I simply moisten the bases of the cuttings, dip them into hormone rooting powder (Fig 2.21), then push them into holes which I have already made with a pencil.

The important thing now is to keep the cuttings damp. I find the best way is to sink the pots into a sand bed in a corner of our polytunnel. This sand a bit of root attached. Peonies, hellebores, cardoon and globe artichokes are all easy to increase in this manner (Fig 2.22). When planting well-rooted peony plants, it is as well to heed some good advice I was given by a professional grower. Never plant them too deep, as they like to have their crowns just above the surface. Also, when feeding or mulching, keep the organic matter away from the crown, it will still sink down to feed the root but leave plenty of air around the plant.

Another method of increasing hellebores is by collecting the seeds when they are ripe, immediately sowing them in pots or trays, and leaving them in an unheated greenhouse or cold frame over winter. They usually grow easily and can sometimes produce interesting colours. Due to cross-pollination by bees, the offspring are seldom the same as the parent plant.

Some shrubs, and often even trees, throw up suckers from around the base, so it is always worthwhile having a good look around for these as, provided they have a tiny piece of root attached, they will usually grow easily. *Kerria japonica* is one that will grow from a piece which is simply pulled off the root system. Others need to be dug out with a bit more care and then severed from the parent with secateurs.

Another method by which shrubs often self-propagate is 'layering'. If a low branch has touched the ground, and maybe been forced lower by moss or summer weeds, it will often be found that the branch has taken root and merely needs digging out and severing. Sharp eyes, and constant vigilance, are needed to discover such treasures!

When planting any of these self-rooted shrubs, it is usually an advantage to pot them up first in compost mixed with a little bonemeal in order that they establish a good root system. They can then be planted in their permanent position during spring or autumn.

For those with patience, there are numerous shrubs, and even trees, that can be grown from seed. It is always worth a try and while some won't germinate, others will. Collect the berries

Fig 2.22
Planting up a peony side shoot

when they are ripe in autumn, and break them open to expose the seeds. I usually leave them for a few days to dry on a paper towel, then sow them in a pot without delay. Cover the seeds lightly with compost and leave the pot outside where it will have the benefit of winter frosts, so as to emulate nature as closely as possible. Germination may take place in the increasing warmth of spring, but if not, don't lose heart. Sink the pot into the ground in a shady place, where it will not dry out, and you could be surprised to find several seedlings by autumn. If they are very tiny at this time, leave the potting on until spring. But if they germinated earlier and are growing strongly, they can be repotted into individual pots and then left in a sheltered spot over winter. Depending upon size, they can usually be planted in the garden after about two years.

The exception to this rule is sweet gum (*Eucalyptus*). In cooler climates the seeds seldom mature fully on the tree and need to be bought. They are very easy to raise when sown in spring, and grow so rapidly that they are often ready for planting outside in mild areas by autumn. But in case of a cold winter, it is usually wiser to leave them in pots and put them in a sheltered spot until the following spring.

Harvesting
AND
Collecting

Harvesting
AND
Collecting

There are few months in the year when plant material cannot be gathered and the secret of successful preservation is knowing exactly when a particular type should be harvested.

Winter

It is hard to believe that material for preserving can be found during these cold months, but in fact there is an abundance throughout the countryside, which is there for the taking. However, I do stress here that any collecting from the wild should be done sparingly so as not to destroy the natural balance.

Holly that has adorned the pictures and mantelpiece over Christmas should already be quite dry and can simply be stored in a dry place then used later to form the basis or background for arrangements. If your Christmas tree was of the blue-pine type, which does not drop its needles, cut off some small branches and store them with the holly. In future years these can be sprayed gold, silver or green and used to make Christmas table decorations.

Ferns growing in shady places are perfect for pressing in mid-winter as they should have reached full maturity but still be a good green. After pressing, this colour will be retained for a long time. The leaves of many evergreen shrubs are at their best for pressing at this time, too. Large individual leaves of *Choisya ternata*, laurel, green ivy and small sprays of bamboo could all be useful later.

For anyone seriously considering flower drying and preserving, it is well worthwhile, in fact almost essential, to have a plentiful supply of sweet gum (*Eucalyptus*). In order to keep the trees small and manageable, they need to be constantly pruned making it feasible to have more than one in a garden. They can then have their tops removed in alternate years, so keeping the trees to a reasonable size and providing plenty of foliage for the dried store. Branches for drying or preserving in glycerine can be cut at almost any time of year, but winter is the best time when, like other evergreens, they are at their most mature, and the new growth has not yet started. A word of warning here. If the pruning is to be extensive, it should only be done during a period of mild weather or the tree may suffer frost damage.

Glycerine preserving needs a little planning as there are so many types of foliage which respond well to the treatment at this time of year. Start with the ones that need the shortest time to absorb the solution. Sprays of *Elaeagnus*, *Euonymus fortunei* and bay can all be removed after 10 to 14 days. Sweet gum (*Eucalyptus*) is usually sufficiently preserved after a week. Mahonia needs a good four to six weeks, and the leaves will gradually turn a wonderful bronze colour. The large leathery leaves of *Fatsia japonica* are easy to preserve as they signal when sufficient glycerine has been absorbed by the central spine turning brown.

The last candidates for the glycerine bucket should be sprays of *Garrya elliptica*, laurel and photinia as their preservation takes several weeks. After treatment, these three make dramatic additions to large displays. *Garrya* leaves turn nearly black and the green tassels become grey, making them a good contrast to green foliage. The other two will become a rich bronze colour.

Sprays of box, myrtle and *Pittosporum* are perfect for drying at this time of year and all three retain their green colour better without glycerine treatment. Simply dry them flat in a warm place.

The flat sword-shaped leaves of *Iris foetidissima*, both green and variegated, can be collected at any time during winter and hung in a warm place to dry in small bunches. They will remain green for a long time and the dried leaves can be used in several ways in arrangements: wired together in small bunches to give definition to the outline of an arrangement, or spilling out at the front and sides.

All types of bright green moss can be found during winter. The damp banks of ditches are a good source for the large sheets, which are so useful for covering the mechanics of dried arrangements. Some woods have ample supplies of bun moss, which is effective for finishing the bases of dried flower trees. Silver grey lichens are often to be found on the ground under trees. Apple trees provide a favourite host for these beautiful filigree-like growths. Sometimes complete lichen-covered branches or twigs will be found and can often be incorporated into arrangements. The small pieces have numerous uses in dried flower decoration and design; for instance, a small piece glued to the stem of a dried flower tree, or mixed together with the moss base, can be very effective.

It is worthwhile keeping a sharp lookout for fungi growing on branches, old wood or log piles. These can be very beautiful and also have a place in many designs. They need to be picked off with care and washed in a mild disinfectant solution in order to kill off any insects they may be harbouring, then put in a warm place to dry out completely before being used.

The tides of winter can throw up a treasure chest of driftwood on some beaches, and a good collection of this is useful in the dried flower store. It will last indefinitely, and if the pieces are chosen carefully they can be found in weird and wonderful shapes, some covered in bumps and knobs, others smooth and shiny, all with that wonderful silvery colour, only achieved after a long period in the sea (Fig 3.1).

To save storage space when you get them home, it is a good idea to cut them, either with a saw or secateurs, into quite short lengths, keeping the most interestingly shaped pieces and discarding the straight bits. For most uses, I seldom need pieces any longer than 30–40cm (12–16in) and these can be incorporated into all sorts of designs. They look particularly effective when incorporated into arrangements as the 'trunks' of dried flower trees.

Fig 3.1 A collection of mosses, lichens and driftwood

Spring

This is the time to begin drying flowers in silica gel in earnest. I first realized that daffodils were suitable for drying when I left some in a vase whilst on holiday. On my return they were paper textured and perfectly dried – albeit rather shrivelled. This is always a good test, and any flower or foliage that dries reasonably well in a vase – without dropping leaves or losing colour – will almost certainly respond well to one or other drying techniques. The best type of daffodils for silica gel treatment are the short-trumpeted ones, flat-faced narcissus types and little miniatures such as the variety 'Téte-â-Téte'. It is best to dry only the heads; but if there is room in your drying box you can push wires into the fat sections behind the heads first and bend them into the same shape as the stems, then lie them in the drying box on a deep bed of desiccant in order to give the petals good support. Next fill the trumpets, and then all around the flowers until they are completely buried.

The reason for not drying the stems is that the process changes them from green to an ugly brown. Unfortunately the same happens to the leaves. If any natural-looking leaves are needed, for instance to put with miniature daffodils in

Fig 3.2 Dried daffodils and camellias beside a bunch of dried buttercups

until next winter. It is surprising just how much can be needed for covering florist's foam in only a few arrangements.

Little dried flower pictures made in recessed frames can be very effective, and one of the best flowers to display in this manner is the hellebore (Fig 3.3). Pick the flowers along with several leaves, keeping the stems as long as possible, and dry them in silica gel. This should not take more than four or five days, and once completely dry they can be reassembled as a natural-looking little bunch in a frame.

Another easily preserved little spring flower is the pansy. When dried in silica gel, these keep their colour perfectly and, with a florists' wire glued to the back, can be used in most small arrangements.

Yellow is the predominant colour of spring and can be collected in all its different shades. *Kerria japonica* flowers look a bit like larkspur when dried. Pick the sprays when most of the flowers are fully out, then make them into

picture frames, use snowdrop leaves instead, which remain green after drying.

Camellia flowers dry beautifully in silica gel, but it is important to remember that although their beautiful clear colours will be unchanged immediately after drying, exposure to air and light will cause them to turn a rusty brown after a while, and this can clash horribly if they are displayed in an arrangement that consists predominantly of pink flowers (Fig 3.2).

All types of hellebores will also dry well in silica gel. They are best gathered when the flowers first come out and the attractive central stamens are to be seen. Either dry only the heads for later wiring, or a more natural look can be achieved if they are dried on their own stems. The green 'Stinking Hellebore' (*Helleborus foetidus*) also dries well by hanging.

It is a good idea to check on the store of moss now, as this is about the last time it will be visible

Fig 3.3 Dried hellebores look wonderful displayed in a frame

Fig 3.4 *Rhodanthe* flowers, which can be arranged to great effect with buttercups

Fig 3.5 A bunch of green honesty heads beside some drying alliums in a basket

bunches and hang them up to dry in a warm place. Keep an eye out for buttercups in fields and wild areas, as the flowers dry well by hanging in bunches and look charming arranged later in pots or baskets together with *Rhodanthe* flowers (Fig 3.4). Both these types will first need wiring into little bunches and the overall effect will resemble an arrangement of freshly picked buttercups and daisies.

Smyrnium olusatrum 'Alexanders' is the strangely named wild flower sometimes to be found during early spring growing in coastal areas of southern England, mainly on roadside verges. It is a bit like cow parsley, but with umbels of yellow-green flowers that dry well when hung in a warm place. They retain an interesting lime-green colour which is particularly effective when used in flower arrangements together with shades of pink. Wild garlic (*Allium ursinum*) is another wild flower that grows on banks and in damp places, and dries easily in the same way as most other alliums (Fig 3.5). The stems poked through small-mesh wire netting stretched over a box or basket is the best method of drying them. The stems are very fragile so they will need to have a wire pushed into them before use.

As spring comes to an end, so lilac starts to bloom. It is well worthwhile picking some sprigs and drying a few bunches in a warm place as the scent lasts almost indefinitely, and though the flowers loose their vibrant colour, they make a very useful and fragrant 'filler' for large arrangements. The silica gel method also works well, though the scent will not be so strong.

Summer

The very first flowers of this season are peonies and both the colour retention and shape of all varieties make them unsurpassed as dried flowers (Figs 3.6 and 3.7). Where possible, they should be picked on a dry day, at exactly the right moment, which is when the flower has just opened and the outer petals are still curved slightly inwards.

Once the flower is fully open and these petals start to turn back, it is too late and they are likely to disintegrate when dried.

The best drying method for peonies is undoubtedly in silica gel. Only dry the heads; push them quite forcibly into the 'bed', pour the desiccant first around each head and then between the petals, making sure all the crevices are filled, with the shape kept as perfect as possible without the petals being crushed. In common with all other flowers, peonies should be put into the crystals as soon as possible after picking, but if the weather is very damp they can be picked on long stems, brought into the house and stood in water until the heads feel dry to the touch. Whatever the weather, give the heads a

Fig 3.6 'Laura Dessert' peony

Fig 3.7 'Bowl of Beauty' peony

Fig 3.8 The 'rounded', 'urn-shaped' and 'rosette-shaped' roses are suitable for drying, whereas the 'high-centred' variety is not

good shake before settling them into their drying box. A surprising amount of moisture accumulates amongst the myriad petals, and any hidden bugs will be jolted out at the same time.

It is also quite possible to air-dry peonies. Pick them as already described and make them into small bunches, about three at a time, before hanging them in a warm place. By this method, they will take quite some time to dry completely, and end up about half their original size.

Hard on the heels of peonies, roses come into their first and best flowering period during early summer. They will of course bloom continually for most of the summer, but the quality of the early ones far surpasses that of later flowerings. Whilst the shape of the flower is important, colour is a factor to consider as well and it is worthwhile knowing that, once dry, they will usually turn a couple of shades deeper. Undoubtedly, the colour that lasts longest in its

dried state is dark red, followed by really strong pink and orange. Some colours, notably the pale yellows, pinks and salmon, turn a nondescript beige after a while, even though they may appear perfect immediately after drying. A few of the true 'buttery' yellows, such as the variety 'Grandpa Dickson', retain their colour reasonably well.

As regards the shape of a rose, avoid any with a tightly furled and pointed centre, which never open completely. Look for those with a perfect shape, the petals slightly parted and the centre still closed (Fig 3.8). Once again, the silica gel method is the ideal way of preserving roses. Treat them in the same way as peonies, but when they are removed from the desiccant it is very important to continue the drying process in a warm place until the seed box and stem at the back of the flower are completely dry, as these always take longer than the petals (Fig 3.9).

It is a good idea to preserve a few roses by
hanging them in a warm place. Dried in this
manner, the effect is quite different from the
fresh look of desiccant drying. The flowers
shrivel to about half their original size and end
up looking like the small dried roses that are
often sold in shops. More interesting results are
to be had by using garden roses of the flat-faced
double types. The varieties 'Garnette' and
'Flower Carpet', some of the small-flowered
rambler types and the shrub rose 'Elmshorn' are
all excellent when dried in this manner. An
alternative is to buy a few bunches of cultivated
roses when they are at their most inexpensive
and hang them up to dry in a warm place, just
as they are, leaves and all. This is much
cheaper than buying them ready-dried, and the
effect of a few air-dried roses mixed in with
those dried in desiccant can give an interesting
variation of textures to dried flower
arrangements (Fig 3.10).

Some books recommend that all roses should
be dried by the hanging method then, once
completely dry, steamed open over a kettle. It is
quite possible to do this, but the work involved
equals that of silica gel drying, the results are
inferior and the flowers will remain crinkled,
never totally regaining their original size.
Steaming can be useful though, when any
flowers become crushed during silica gel drying.
The best way to do this is to attach a wire 'stem',
steam the flower upside down, then leave it
hanging so that the petals fall back into their
correct shape or, in the case of flat-faced flowers
such as *Rudbeckia*, standing upright until once
again completely dry.

Early summer is a good time to preserve the
leaves of Solomon's seal; immediately the small
white flowers are over, pick plenty of the arching
sprays, bunch and hang them in a warm place
and they will give you long-lasting green leaves for
outlining large displays. Beware of waiting too
long before picking them or you may find that the
leaves have been devoured by sawflies.

Fig 3.9 A rose and a peony at the right stage for drying in
silica gel

Fig 3.10 A rose of the type most suitable for drying by
hanging

Fig 3.11 Hangers with drying delphiniums, along with *Euphorbia* and *Persicaria*

Acanthus, with its long spires, is another useful flower for forming the basis of large arrangements. Wait until the majority of flowers are fully out to pick them; like delphiniums the lower ones will be over by this stage. They should be made into bunches of no more than five stems and hung to dry in the air (Fig 3.11). The best thing about these flowers is the attractive shapes they grow into, and with their pale colour they will add grace and charm to many different types of flower arrangement.

Due to their texture, *Echinops*, *Eryngium* and teasel are useful additions to the dried flower store as their exotic appearance makes a total contrast to the more conventional flowers. *Echinops* are ready for picking when at their most steely blue, that is, before the little flowers which form each head have actually come out. If they are left until after flowering, the colour will fade and they will disintegrate once dry. *Eryngium* needs to be harvested when the heads are well developed and a good silver or blue colour, depending on the type. I like to pick teasel when the heads are green, and this, like the other two, dries easily standing in jars or made into bunches and hung up.

All members of the *Achillea* family, from wild yarrow to the border varieties, should be gathered in quantity as they are easy to dry by simply hanging in the air. To do this successfully, make sure that all the tiny flowers on each head are fully out before picking. *Centaurea macrocephala* is another flower that is easy to dry, as is *Solidago* (golden rod). The former can be picked just as soon as the little yellow tufts appear on their heads, and golden rod makes a really useful 'filler' when gathered both in bud (still green) and later when the flowers are fully out and a good yellow. It must not be left too late or the flowers will turn brown.

Once the perennials start flowering it seems as if all their buds burst at the same moment, therefore the picking needs to be done on a daily basis. One of the earliest is *Alchemilla mollis*. The little greenish-yellow flowers are ready for harvesting just as soon as they come out fully. They can be made into fairly fat bunches as they dry easily. For the best results this should be done quickly in a warm place.

Keep an eye on your delphiniums; they can be enjoyed in the garden until flowering is nearly over, but the moment to pick them for drying is as soon as the lower flowers on the spike come to an end and there are still a few buds at the top. Hang them individually in a warm place to dry.

If you have a few stately cardoon plants in your garden, and can spare some of the flower heads for drying, be sure to cut them just as soon as the purple tufts appear on their heads – leave them too long and once dry they will disintegrate. However, this need not be a total disaster, as once the outer petals fall away, what is left is a large silky white seed-head which can also have its uses. Sometimes it is nice to pick these flowers even before they open, in the tightly closed bud stage which dries just as easily. The stems are very thick and heavy, so keep them quite short, about 30cm (12in), then hang them individually with an 'S' hook in the same manner as delphiniums. Even more dramatic than cardoon are globe artichokes, if they can be spared from the table. They, too, must be picked as soon as the blue heads appear. Before use, lengthen the existing stems by pushing in two or three heavy-gauge florists' wires, or a sharpened plant stick.

The vegetable and herb garden needs careful watching. Chive flowers are at their best for drying when they are fully out with a good strong pink colour. Marjoram, too, should be gathered when the flowers are fully out. Both the pink- and red-flowered types are invaluable for use as fillers in many different arrangements. I now grow a large clump of leeks as perennials in the cutting border – for the flowers rather than the vegetable, as they are invaluable for adding to large arrangements. They can be picked once the flowers are fully out and have just started to set seed; dry them standing upright in a warm place. The process will take several weeks to complete and, be warned, they give off a strong onion scent.

Dahlias are one of the most reliable summer flowers for preserving in silica gel, as they invariably dry perfectly and keep their colour for many years. The best flowers to use are the round-shaped, many-faceted types. Only the heads need to be dried; pick them when they first come out and the central disc can barely be

seen. Before use they will have to be wired in the same way as peonies. It is possible to dry the single-flowered and cactus types, but they are nowhere near as successful.

Before leaving the subject of perennials that are good for drying, I must mention two little plants that are really excellent. *Anaphalis* flowers abundantly, dries easily and remains pure white. As the stems are quite fragile, the easiest method of using the flowers in arrangements is to wire together two or three of the heads with their clusters of flowers, then use the wire in place of the stems. The little spiky flowers of the different types of *Persicaria* are most attractive as they cover a spectrum of colours from palest pink to deep red and flower on and off all summer. They are best dried in a warm place then wired in the same way as *Anaphalis* before use.

As summer progresses, the autumn- and spring-sown annuals will come into flower. One of the first is *Nigella*, which is generally grown for its attractive green seed-heads. The pale blue and white flowers can also be dried either by hanging or in silica gel, but sadly the colours are not long-lasting. The best moment to pick them is just as soon as there are plenty of big fat seed-heads on each stem. If they are gathered green, they will remain so, whereas those that are left on the plant for too long will turn a pinky-brown. Annual poppies will flower during most of the summer, and the seedheads can be gathered as soon as they are mature and the colour is just turning from green to grey.

Larkspur is a very economical flower for drying if it is picked with care. As each plant consists of a central spike, which is surrounded by numerous others in the bud stage, it is quite possible to cut just the flowering spike, leaving the buds to come out for further picking later on. The stems can easily be lengthened by pushing a wire into them before use. This also has the advantage of enabling the stems to be bent into more natural shapes, otherwise larkspur can be very stiff and straight. It is always nice to have a few dried buds as well as the flowers, but this can be left until the last of the flower spikes is collected.

The strawflower (*Helichrysum*) is another flower that is usually grown specifically for drying, though they also make a splendid splash of colour wherever they bloom. The heads can be harvested just as soon as the first two or three layers of outer petals have opened fully. If the flowers are left on the plant until their centres are showing, this is too late, as they continue to open during drying and the centre will then go to seed, causing the flower to shatter.

The reason for picking only the heads is in order to wire them in their fresh state. Of course they can be dried on their natural stems, but the problem with this is that they are very fragile, also the heads tend to turn downwards. Wiring is a very simple operation; push a florist's wire firmly into the back of the head where the stem has been cut off and, holding a finger on the top of the flower as a guide, make sure the wire does not protrude through the centre. If it does come through, simply pull it back a fraction. The wired flowers can now be put in a warm place to dry, either standing in jars or in blocks of florists' foam. As the heads dry, they will adhere firmly to the wires and be ready for use in arrangements.

Statice (*Limonium*) is another of the 'paper-textured' types of flower, but in this case wait until all the little trumpet-shaped flowers in a spray are fully out. They will not open any further during drying, so any that are picked in bud will remain in that state. They feel almost dry and papery when they are picked, so merely bunch them and hang them in any airy spot.

Any grasses that are to be used for drying should be picked as soon as their heads emerge. Those with dangling heads such as quaking grass should be dried standing upright. Use baskets for this, not glass or plastic containers, or the stems may develop mould. The upright types can all be dried hanging in bunches, and

a warm place will ensure that they remain as green as possible. In the same category, though not strictly a grass, wheat should be dried with great care. In the past, I have learnt to my cost that it has a very high moisture content that easily creates mildew, so the size of bunches should be kept small, then dried in as warm a place as possible.

Both green and red amaranthus are ready for picking when the first tiny brown seeds can be seen on the flower spikes. They must be watched carefully, for if they are picked too early, the stems will be weak; leave them too late and they will lose their brilliant green and red colours. Hang them in bunches to dry in a warm place in order to preserve the colours.

The daisy-like flowers of *Rhodanthe* and *Ammobium* both need slightly different treatment. You can cut just the flowering stems of *Ammobium*, leaving plenty of buds to flower later. In the case of *Rhodanthe*, it is usually easiest to cut the whole plant in order to have a good selection of buds and flowers. Both of these dry well, hanging in bunches in any airy place.

Due to my fondness for green in dried flower arrangements, I always grow plenty of *Carthamus* and *Moluccella*. I like to pick the former just as soon as one or more stems on each plant are showing coloured tufts. In this way, there will also be plenty of useful green buds branching off the main stem. They dry easily in bunches and though not essential, a warm place helps to retain the colour. *Moluccella*, on the other hand, should not be harvested until it is quite mature and the little flowers in the centre of each 'bell' are over. To prevent the calyces becoming too brittle after drying, the sprays should be given glycerine treatment for three or four days, and then they can be bunched and hung in a warm place.

The tall spikes of *Atriplex* also fall into the green category even though they will be deep red when picked. After hanging to dry for a while, they will gradually turn green.

Zinnia, African marigolds and *Rudbeckia* are some of the most spectacular of the larger flowers; all three are best dried in silica gel, as they then retain their shape and fresh colour. Dry only the heads and use a glue gun to wire them later. There is an easy way to tell when *Zinnia* flowers are at their best for preserving; a ring of 'stars' gradually develops around the flower's centre, and when this circle is complete they can be picked. African marigolds should be fully open but not overblown before picking; they are very fleshy flowers and can take from 10 to 14 days to dry completely. *Rudbeckia* heads should be gathered just as soon as they open fully, and not left in silica gel for longer than a week or the petals may drop off. Later on, when the petals on those left in the garden have died back, the black flower centres can be collected and dried too, as they often add a useful contrast to the other colours in arrangements.

Late summer is the time for preserving sprays of beech leaves in glycerine. It is important to pick them before they start to change colour or they will be unable to absorb the glycerine solution. Look for sprays that are undamaged by insects or disease.

Autumn

So often the drying of hydrangeas proves to be a disappointment and I am constantly being told of the total failure some people experience with these magnificent heads. The usual problem is that they are picked too early when they are still showing their first bright colours, and the only way to dry them in this state is in silica gel, but the colour will then not last well. It is better to wait until their colour has changed almost entirely to a slightly softer shade, and the bracts that form the familiar 'flower heads' feel slightly leathery to the touch; a useful guide is to look for the actual flowers, a tiny spider-like scrap in the centre of each bract, as while these are still visible it is too early to pick them. The heads can

then either be dried in a warm place by hanging in small bunches or put into water and left there until they feel quite crisp and dry. When picking hydrangeas, it is important to remember that next year's blooms depend upon the buds that can already be seen, so either cut them with short stems for bunching, or cut only the heads, then tie four or five long strings to a wire clothes hanger and attach the heads to the strings with clothes-pegs. In this way a large quantity of heads can be dried in a small space. It is an easy matter to give them false stems after drying by simply pushing a stout florists' wire into the remaining portion of stem.

Flower beds continue to provide plentiful material until well into autumn, in fact some plants dry better for being left as late as possible. *Ballota,* for instance, is a plant that will provide you with quantities of attractive and unusual sprays for drying, and should be picked when the little rosettes which encircle the stems are well formed and firm. The colour should still be a good silver-grey and they will then dry easily hanging in an airy place.

Montbretia is another flower that is at its best in late summer. It dries surprisingly well, and the pretty arching sprays add lightness to arrangements, combined with an interesting colour. They can be gathered when the lower flowers have started to die back and there are plenty of buds still on the spray. They are best dried by hanging in bunches in a warm place.

Clary and *Nicandra* are two more types that should be left as late as possible before picking. Keep an eye on the *Clary* bracts, and when they still have a good colour and feel fairly crisp to the touch, bunch and dry them in a warm place. If your *Nicandra* plants have self-seeded, it is often well into autumn before they are ready for picking. Wait until as many olive-green bells as possible have formed, then gather the whole plants and hang them individually in an airy place.

Carline thistles are wonderful when dried, each head like a shimmering white sun. They can be left on the plant until well into autumn, then picked with as long a stem as possible. The easiest way to dry them is to push a florists' wire into each stem, form the end into a hook, then hang them individually from a wire hanger. Once dry, the brown seeds can be rubbed off the centre of the flowers as they are more attractive when pure white.

As a rule, the last splash of autumn colour in flower borders will be provided by Chinese lanterns, *Iris foetidissima* and Michaelmas daisies. The latter are not ideal for drying as they become considerably reduced in size but at the same time, if they are picked when they are fully out and made into small bunches then hung in a warm place, they retain excellent colour and can make a useful filler for dried arrangements. Chinese lanterns on the other hand, though often scorned for their old-fashioned image, can be one of the most colourful and texturally interesting additions to arrangements. When used with care and imagination, their attractive and interesting shapes can create dramatic effects (Fig 3.12). They should be left for as long as possible before harvesting, so that the maximum amount of 'lanterns' have turned to brilliant orange/scarlet – even if the lower ones have started to turn brown as these can easily be snipped off before use. They dry easily hanging in bunches in any airy spot. There is another use for these spectacular plants; any that are left in the garden through the winter may well skeletonize naturally into delightful filigree bells with a bright orange berry in the centre of each one. *Iris foetidissima* can be gathered as soon as the scarlet seed-filled pods open up. Spray

each one with a special 'surface sealer' or hairspray to fix the berries and hang them in bunches to dry in a warm place.

Gourds and ornamental maize can be collected through the season as they become fully ripe. Maize dries easily lying or standing upright in a warm place. Unfortunately the English climate is not suitable for drying gourds successfully, so I usually just pile them into a dish to make an attractive ornament. In this way, some will dry in a warm room, though with loss of colour, others will probably turn mouldy after a few months and can then be thrown out.

The last of the garden flowers to be harvested will probably be pampas grass. The plumes are a bit big to be of great use except in very large arrangements, but they can always be broken down into shorter lengths. Drying is simple; pick them as soon as possible after the plumes emerge for if they are left too long they will shed like moulting dogs. They dry easily, standing in a bucket or any large container.

Hedgerows, too, can be a rich source of autumn material. Look out for hops, 'Old Man's Beard' and rosehips. Hops can be collected as soon as the flowers are well formed and are a good green colour. If hung in a warm place to dry they will retain their colour for a long while. 'Old Man's Beard' can either be picked when it bears silky trusses, which preserve well in glycerine, or wait until they turn fluffy, then spray them with hairspray or a special sealer and store them in a warm place. Rosehips together with their leaves can be preserved in glycerine too, as can other berries such as *Cotoneaster* and *Pyracantha*.

Fig 3.12 An autumnal wall hanging made on a plait using *Rudbeckia* heads with shells, 'bread rolls', wheat, hops and Chinese lanterns

ARRANGING

Preserved Material

ARRANGING
Preserved Material

When displayed in baskets and vases, dried flowers and foliage can be as colourful and striking as the fresh variety, but with the added advantage of their long-lasting qualities.

Before embarking on any arrangements it will be necessary to collect together a few useful tools (Fig 4.1). The following items are those that you will need initially.

EQUIPMENT

Florists' grey 'dry' foam blocks
(this type of foam should always be used for dried work rather than the green fresh flower foam, which does not always hold the material firmly enough when used in its dry state)

Florists' wires

Glue gun

Secateurs for cutting both stems and wire

Green and brown floral tape for wrapping wires (this should be the type intended for dried material, not the waterproof variety used in fresh flower floristry)

'Frogs' and fixing putty (these are spiked plastic holders that are fixed into the base of a container with the putty in order to hold the foam firmly from below)

Green, white or clear adhesive tape for holding foam in place

Knife

Turntable (useful but not essential)

Special protective spray for flowers dried in silica gel (hairspray can be used).

Fig 4.1 A selection of useful tools for making dried flower arrangements

Selection of containers

Dried flowers can look good in almost any container once the knack of arranging them in a natural manner has been mastered. They lend themselves to baskets, pottery, china and even glass. Often a chosen container will provide inspiration for the colour and shape of an arrangement.

Fig 4.2 The colour of this vase provided inspiration for the shades of flowers used in the arrangement

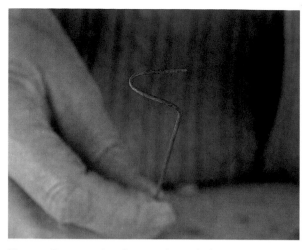

Fig 4.3 Forming a 'U' shape at the end of a piece of wire

Fig 4.4 Applying some hot glue to the back of a flower head

Wiring flowers

It seems somewhat of a contradiction, but in order to look more natural, most dried flowers will require wiring before they are used in arrangements. Unless they already have curved shapes, the effect of drying will make them very stiff and straight, so in order to give them that 'just picked' look they need to be moulded and bent into the sort of shapes they have when fresh. Anything with a hollow stem, such as larkspur, can have a florists' wire pushed as far in as possible. For this purpose, 19-gauge wires will be adequate, but your store should also contain some of the heavier 18 gauge, and for fine work and delicate flowers, 22 gauge. The thicker one is essential for heavy heads such as peonies and cardoons as well as for pushing into the hollow stems of delphiniums.

To wire the head of a flower that has been dried in silica gel, bend the top of the wire into a small 'U' shape (Fig 4.3), bend that over so that it is flat on top, then using a glue gun, attach the 'U' to the back of the flower where the stalk would normally be (Fig 4.4), and hold it in place until it sets (Fig 4.5). The wire can then either have a

Fig 4.5 Gluing the wire stalk to the flower head

Fig 4.6 Slipping a wheat stem over the wire

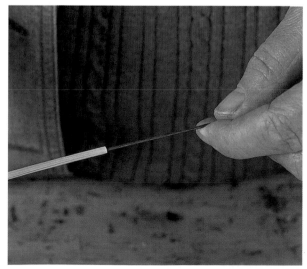

hollow grass or wheat stem slipped over it (Fig 4.6), or be wrapped with floral tape. When doing this it is easiest to hold the tape taut in one hand and turn the wire, ensuring that it is as tight as possible (Fig 4.7).

Another use for wiring is to bunch together several small flowers, or sprigs of foliage, in order that they make a greater impact in an arrangement. To do this, once again bend the top of the wire into a 'U' shape, but longer this time (Fig 4.8). Holding the bunch of flower stems in one hand with the 'U' shape against it, twist the long end of the wire around both the short end and the bunch, making sure the wires are tightly twisted together below the bunch (Fig 4.9). If this wire 'stem' needs lengthening before use, hold a straight wire against the flower stem so that it too is held in place by the two twisted ones. This technique is quite hard on the fingers if done properly, but it gives the most secure hold to any dried material and it can be used in just the same way for lengthening stems of any sort. When using a heavy stem, it is best to wire it on to a strong plant stick. If the wires are going to show in an arrangement, cover the top part with floral tape (Fig 4.10).

Fig 4.7 Wrapping the wire with floral tape

Fig 4.8 Holding a bunch of larkspur ready for wiring

Fig 4.9 Securing the bunch with the wire

Fig 4.10 Covering the wired bunch with tape

Preparing containers

Once your flowers are wired and ready, start preparing your chosen container by cutting grey florists' foam to fit in it as tightly as possible, making sure that it comes to about 4cm (1½in) above the rim of the container. Fix a 'frog' to the base of your vase and push the foam firmly on to it. Use narrow adhesive tape to hold the foam firmly in place by stretching it across the top in two directions, or in the case of a basket, twine stretched between the handles. Cover the foam all over with moss which can be held in place using short lengths of wire bent into hairpin shapes.

If you are making a 'one-sided' arrangement to stand against a wall, it may be necessary to add some weight to the back of the container as wired flowers are quite heavy and may cause it to tip forward. You can either push a heavy stone down between the foam and vase edge or hang a special florist's weight on the back.

Using foliage

Before you start putting any flowers into your container, use dried and preserved foliage to create the desired shape and provide a green background to the arrangement. It is surprising just how much foliage is needed to completely fill a container but it is worthwhile doing the job thoroughly as you will need far less flowers than you would without the foliage. Once the shape is in place flowers can be added. For a really natural look it may be necessary to poke in some more foliage as a final touch, maybe a few sprigs of eucalyptus wired together or some green flowers such as *Ballota* or *Nicandra* to spill over the edges.

Arranging dried flowers

With a good store of preserved material, you have a whole world of flower arranging possibilities at your fingertips. From stark modern displays to glorious opulent studies in the manner of Dutch

Old Master painters. In fact, copies of many of these pictures such as *Vase of Flowers* by Jacob van Walscapelle (National Gallery) are well worth studying as they often show in the most superb detail exactly how a flower grows naturally. With the use of wires and false stems dried flowers can be moulded into similar shapes.

The celebrated gardener and flower arranger, Constance Spry, used to exhort her pupils to pick their fresh flowers for arranging in the most interesting and flowing shapes that they could find. The same applies to the dried variety. Any that are picked with bends and curves in their stems should be dried exactly as they are and can then be used to great effect in appropriate displays.

It is important for people to follow their own individual style when making arrangements and to remember that the simple rules of fresh flower arranging apply equally to dried flowers. For instance, that except in the case of some modern designs, the height of the flowers should be approximately two and a half times that of the container, that all the material should appear to spring from a central point in your vase, and that strong colours should be grouped together to make bold blocks rather than be scattered throughout. With this in mind, along with a good supply of wired flowers and plenty of dried foliage, anybody should be able to create attractive winter displays.

Unusual ways of using dried flowers

It is a mistake to think of preserved flowers purely as components of conventional flower arrangements. With imagination, they can be used as design tools in many different ways. A tree shape is one of the most effective ways of displaying dried flowers and makes an attractive decoration for many different situations. These are often made using the 'ball on a stick' method, the stick usually being a piece of dowelling wrapped with ribbons. A more natural, and I think attractive, look is achieved when the 'tree trunk' is formed from one or more pieces of driftwood or interestingly shaped branches (see page 64).

A plain straw hat can easily be transformed into a stunning creation suitable for smart race meetings and summer weddings. Simply wrap a long ivy strand (with the leaves removed) around the crown, wire it firmly into place, then use a glue gun to fix dried peonies, larkspur and sweet gum (*Eucalyptus*) leaves on to the ivy as if they were growing from it (Fig 4.11).

Massed strawflowers (*Helichrysum brachteatum*) in a single colour always look dramatic as each colour group consists of such an array of shades. Use them to great effect to entirely cover a hat, both crown and brim, fixing

the flowers in place with a glue gun. Use shades of yellow and orange, glued to a cardboard base in the shape of a rising sun, or experiment with different colours on toy shapes to hang on a child's bedroom wall (see page 76).

A natural wheatsheaf is another attractive card-based wall decoration, or it can be made as a larger version that can be used as a firescreen during the summer months. Even if these are made with wheat in its green state, after a while it will turn a wonderful shade of harvest gold (see page 79).

There is no reason for a winter bride not to have a bouquet made from garden flowers that have been carefully dried during summer and

Fig 4.11 A simple straw hat becomes a romantic creation when decorated with two large peonies, sweet gum leaves, larkspur and *Helichrysum*

Fig 4.12 Gluing the dried leaves to a card

stored in a warm, dark place until needed. With care and imagination, it is possible to make wedding bouquets and headdresses that are hard to distinguish from fresh; and of course they have the added advantage of being long-lasting keepsakes (see pages 69 and 73).

A bride who prefers to carry fresh flowers, can have the best of both worlds if these are subsequently dried and then framed to make a picture. The drying process needs to be carried out whilst the flowers are as fresh as possible. It is essential to take the bouquet apart first and then dry roses, freesias, lilies, orchids and so on in silica gel. Most of the foliage can either be dried in a warm place or pressed, and any gypsophila will dry easily hanging in an airing cupboard or boiler room. Of course, if you have enough silica gel, you can use it to dry everything and this will speed the process up.

When the entire bouquet is completely dry, including time in an airing cupboard to finish the process after any silica gel drying, lay the flowers out roughly on a piece of card to see what size and shape of frame would best suit them. Most picture framers will be willing to build a box on the back of your chosen frame but be sure to ask them to make it deep enough to accommodate the largest flowers with room to spare or they will look squashed.

To complete your frame, either cut a piece of coloured card to size as the background or cover the card with material in a good colour to show off the flowers to best effect. It may also be necessary to paint the inner sides of the 'box' to tone in with the chosen background. When the frame is ready, start by arranging the foliage in an attractive shape on the backing board. Then when you are satisfied with the arrangement, fix each piece in place with colourless glue (Fig 4.12). Next, place the flowers amongst the foliage roughly where you want them then glue them into place (Fig 4.13).

Fig 4.13 Adding the flowers

Fig 4.14 The finished framed bouquet

It is generally better not to use a glue gun for this operation, as the glue tends to leave cobweb-like strands which are hard to remove.

Once the glue has set and all the components are firmly fixed, pick up the board and holding it face down gently shake it to make sure nothing is loose. Check that there are no unsightly areas on the flowers – if any glue is showing for instance, it can be disguised with an extra leaf or bud. Clean the glass carefully before reassembling the frame as it will be difficult to do so later, then using a glue gun, quickly spread a thin layer of glue all the

way round the back of the frame and immediately stick on the backing board with the flowers in place. Check that nothing has moved and then secure the back with strong adhesive tape. Two screw 'eyes' can then be attached at each side with wire or cord between them for hanging the picture.

This makes a lovely wedding memento. It is not necessary for the arrangement to be an exact replica of the bouquet; some of the flowers may well have been damaged anyway. The main thing is to have a lasting keepsake made with at least some of the bridal flowers (Fig 4.14).

Christmas decorations

Artificial green decorations are very popular, and from a distance, it is hard to distinguish them from fresh green pine. But to achieve a more natural look that will last from one year to the next, I break all my rules and do some dyeing! When coloured green, *Statice dumosa* can be used as a base to make all sorts of attractive decorations. The secret to a natural look is to use two or more different shades of green, one a dark pine colour and one or two more of a slightly lighter colour. Each batch is dyed separately then used mixed together in the decorations. Use ordinary household dyes and follow the manufacturers' instructions on heating the dye. As well as the recommended salt, I like to sprinkle in a little detergent as this helps the absorption of the dye, and for good measure, splash in some vinegar too. It will take about 20 minutes to dye each batch and they can then be hung up to dry either outside or over thick batches of newspaper.

The colour lasts for years, so it is worthwhile dyeing as large a bunch in each different shade as you can, then raid the store each Christmas if you want to make new decorations. This type of dyeing is only suitable for making decorations to be used indoors; outdoor wreaths are best made from non-dyed material.

For long swags to hang over a mantelpiece, use the dyed *Statice dumosa* to make up lots of little bunches, wired as described earlier. Then, using a reel of thin wire or string, attach them firmly to a length of rope with a ring attached to each end (Fig 4.15), not forgetting to change the direction of the bunches in the centre (Fig 4.16), so that you end up at the other end with an outward-facing bunch. This will leave a small gap in the middle which can be filled by attaching some fir cones, either with a glue gun or wires (4.17). To complete the swag, glue in at intervals more fir cones and, if possible, some larch cones

together with their twigs, tiny alder cones, mock holly berries, nuts, chestnuts, cinnamon sticks, bows or even some artificial decorations.

Use the green *Statice dumosa* to make table decorations with candles, using grey florists' foam glued to a piece of cork or wood and special plastic candleholders pushed into it. Fill any gaps with moss then add cones and nuts as before. A nice variation is to spray some of these and some pieces of dried hydrangea head with gold paint, and then add them to your arrangement.

Natural decorations can be made for the Christmas tree, too. Using the smallest size of florists' foam ball, make a loop of ribbon or leaf of *Iris foetidissima* and attach it to the ball with a wire, glue *Helichrysum brachteatum* heads over the whole ball and finally spray it gold all over. A number of these make very effective tree decorations.

Christmas is a good time to sort out collections of dried material, as anything that looks old and tired can be given a new lease of life by spraying with gold or silver paint. Holly and mistletoe from the previous year, linseed, poppy and *Nigella* seed-heads, gourds, hops and the tufted heads of carthamus, besides many types of grasses and wheat make invaluable additions to arrangements.

Old hydrangea heads, too, look wonderful when sprayed green then given a light dusting of gold or silver. All these techniques are effective in making imaginative decorations – from large displays to small table-centres – to give away as gifts.

If readers are inspired to try their hand at this fascinating and fulfilling pastime, whether it be merely growing flowers, harvesting and drying what you have in your garden, or even buying flowers ready-dried in order to make your own displays, may you get from it as much pleasure as I do. Take time to wonder at the shape, markings and colour of each petal, and enjoy holding on to the beauty of your flowers for longer than nature intended.

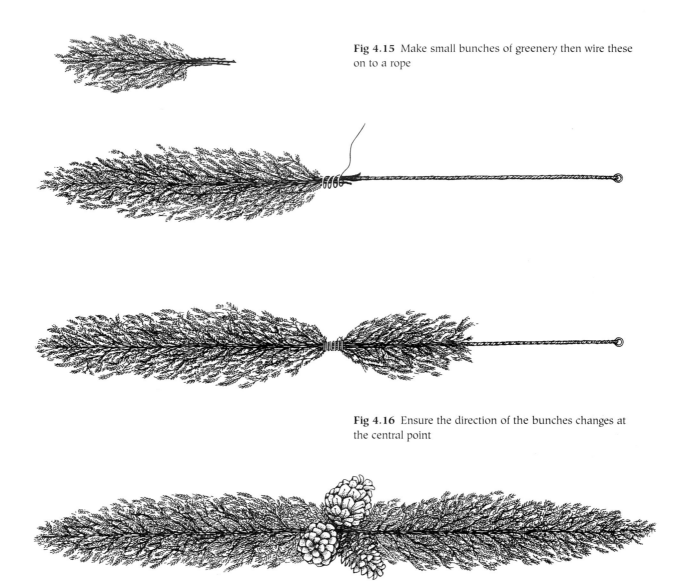

Fig 4.15 Make small bunches of greenery then wire these on to a rope

Fig 4.16 Ensure the direction of the bunches changes at the central point

Fig 4.17 Cover the gap left where the bunches change direction with three large cones

Those lucky enough to possess a garden will be able to empathise with the added joys I find in watching the annual miracle of sprouting seeds and the new life taken on by a rooting cutting, as it transforms from a dry twig to a healthy plant. All this, plus the privilege of being surrounded by sweet scents, first when harvesting the fresh flowers, then later, by the pervading fragrance that fills a warm room where dried flowers hang or are displayed.

Floral Arrangement

PROJECTS

Easy Basket
ARRANGEMENT

*I*f your garden does not contain many flowers suitable for silica gel drying, an equally colourful arrangement can be made with a few air-dried annuals, using *Statice dumosa* as a background, then finishing with some form of green foliage.

Fig 5.1 Securing a piece of florists' foam with a 'frog' in the base of a basket

Fig 5.2 Twine tied between the handles holds the foam in place

Fig 5.3 Covering the foam with moss

MATERIALS AND EQUIPMENT

Basket

Plastic 'frog' and fixing putty

Block of grey florists' foam

String

Moss

Larkspur

Statice dumosa

Wired strawflowers (*Helichrysum bracteatum*), and, if possible, about 5 roses and/or peonies (also wired)

Green amaranthus or ornamental grass

Some sprigs of box or similar foliage with small leaves

Fig 5.4 Adding 'spiky' flowers first

Fig 5.5 Building up the arrangement with strawflowers and peonies

Method

Start by cutting the foam to a suitable size, then fix it to the base of the basket with a 'frog' (Fig 5.1). Tie string between the handles to hold it in place (Fig 5.2). Cover the foam with moss as already described (Fig 5.3), use *Statice dumosa* to form the shape, add 'spiky'-type flowers to start with (Fig 5.4), then strawflowers and peonies or roses (Fig 5.5). Lastly, poke in some green sprigs to spill over the edges.

Large Formal
ARRANGEMENT

A round table in a hall or sitting room makes the ideal setting for a large 'all round' arrangement made with colourful summer flowers.

Fig 5.6 Taping the fixed foam firmly across the top

Fig 5.7 Using moss to cover the foam

Fig 5.8 Create a framework to cover the display

Fig 5.9 Adding clusters of small flowers

MATERIALS AND EQUIPMENT

Bowl or container approximately 30cm
(12in) in diameter

Two blocks of grey florists' foam

White, green or clear tape

Plastic 'frog' and fixing putty

Florists' wires

Moss

Large bunch of eucalyptus and other foliage

Green and red amaranthus

Cream carthamus

Pink larkspur

Light and dark blue larkspur

Shades of pink, purple and blue statice
(*Limonium*)

Phlomis seed-heads

Pink pokers

Wired pink strawflowers (*Helichrysum brachteatum*)

12 ready-wired peonies

10 ready-wired *zinnias*

Method

Cut the foam to a suitable size, fix it in place with the frog and tape it firmly across the top (Fig 5.6), then cover it all over with moss as already described (Fig 5.7). Make a framework with foliage and green amaranthus (Fig 5.8), then bunch together small flowers such as larkspur, statice and pink pokers and add them to the foliage (Fig 5.9). Put the large flowers into place, then add other smaller flowers. Finally, add more foliage to finish the arrangement.

Dried Flower
TREE

A tree shape is a very attractive way of
displaying dried material and can be used as
a decoration in many different situations. They look
good on small tables, and due to their shape, have
the advantage of leaving space around them for
books and photographs.

Fig 5.10 A flowerpot filled with florists' foam

Fig 5.11 Using hot glue to fix pieces of driftwood in place

MATERIALS AND EQUIPMENT

Glue gun

Flowerpot

Driftwood or other twigs

Grey foam block

Grey foam ball (circumference approximately the same as the pot)

Driftwood or other twigs

Moss

Foliage sprays of sweet gum (*Eucalyptus*) and bottlebrush (*Callistemon*)

Seed-heads of *Nigella*

Hops (*Humulus*)

Nicandra

Green amaranthus

Montbretia (*Crocosmia*)

Seed-heads of *Phlomis*

Orange 'pom-pom' dahlias

Lady's mantle (*Alchemilla mollis*)

Chinese lanterns

Wired salmon roses

Green and orange *Carthamus*

Wired orange and yellow strawflowers (*Helichrysum brachteatum*)

Allium siculum seed-heads

Method

Fix a piece of foam into the pot using a glue gun (Fig 5.10). If the container needs extra weight, put some Dry Hard or stones in the bottom first. Cut the wood for the trunk into short lengths. For good proportions it is best not to have them too long. I used a 26cm (10¼ in) piece as the longest. Push them into the foam, then when you are satisfied with the shape, fix them with the glue gun (Fig 5.11).

Fig 5.12 Attach half a foam ball to the top of the stems

Fig 5.13 Covering the foam ball with moss

Fig 5.14 Use foliage to make a tree shape

Fig 5.15 Adding flowers to the foliage

Cut the foam ball in half and fix that to the top of the stems, attaching it with the glue gun as before (Fig 5.12). Cover the half foam ball all over with moss, holding it in place with short pieces of wire bent into hairpin shapes (Fig 5.13). Form the outline of the tree shape by using the sprays of leaves and green amaranthus (Fig 5.14), then begin adding flowers including the Chinese lanterns.

Once they are in place, start filling in the gaps with the remaining materials. (The nigella seed-heads are easier to deal with when wired into small bunches.) Lastly, make little bunches of *Alchemilla* and montbretia and push these in at intervals around the whole tree (Fig 5.15). Cover the foam in the pot with moss held in place either with pins or glue (Fig 5.16). The overall finished height of the tree is approximately 53cm (21in).

Fig 5.16 Using moss to cover the foam in the pot

Hand-tied Arrangement
IN A GLASS VASE

*B*y using a few simple tricks, a loose
arrangement of the type often used to display fresh
flowers can easily be made with dried materials.

Fig 5.17 Placing bound wheat stems into a vase

Fig 5.18 Filling in around the bunch with larkspur stems

Fig 5.19 Pushing in the sweet gum sprays

Method

Start by cleaning the ragged pieces from the wheat stems then put a rubber band, not too tightly, around the top of the bunch. This is to hold it firmly together and also to allow space for the extra stems. Cut the stems so that they stand about 4cm (1½in) higher than the top of the vase, then place the bunch in the centre of the vase (Fig 5.17). Holding it in place with one hand, push in the larkspur stems, one by one, all the way around the bunch (Fig 5.18).

Fig 5.20 Adding larkspur and white achillea

MATERIALS AND EQUIPMENT
Glass vase
Large bunch of wheat stems
Rubber band
Small bunch of (long) larkspur stems
Several sweet gum (*Eucalyptus*) sprays
White achillea
Bunch of blue larkspur
7 ready-wired peonies

Next, start making a natural-looking arrangement by first pushing the sweet gum sprays into the stem bunch (Fig 5.19), then the larkspur and achillea and lastly the wired peonies (Fig 5.20). Make sure the foliage and flowers spill over the top of the vase and hide the bunch of wheat stems.

Wedding Bouquet

*D*ried bouquets look more natural if the flowers are fixed into a foam holder. It is possible to buy these ready-made, or better still, make your own as shown here.

Fig 5.21 Push the wire 'handle' through a foam ball and form hooks that are pulled back into the foam

Fig 5.22 Wrapping the foam ball with wire netting and wiring it to the handle

MATERIALS AND EQUIPMENT

Glue gun

50cm (19¾in) piece of strong plastic-covered wire (the type used for fencing)

10cm (4in) grey foam ball

Small piece of plastic-covered wire netting (3cm (1¼in) mesh)

Cotton wool

Gauze bandage

Satin ribbon: white, or coloured to tone with the flowers

19-gauge florists' wires

Green and brown florists' tape

Moss

PVA glue

Viburnum macrocephalum and *plicatum*

Foliage sprays of sweet gum (*Eucalyptus*)

White larkspur

Sprays of white lilac flowers

White hyacinths

Sprays of bird cherry flowers

3 cream carnations

5 pale pink hellebores

7 pale pink peonies

7 white or cream roses

Method

Fold the thick wire in half, push the two ends through the foam ball (Fig 5.21) and turn back about 4cm (1½in) so that they are firmly embedded in the foam. Now cover the foam ball with wire netting and wire it firmly to the 'handle' (Fig 5.22). Cover the ball with moss, and pin it firmly into place, then cover the handle with cotton wool which is held in place by binding it with fine wire or string (Fig 5.23). Bend the handle slightly, making sure that the angle is right for holding it comfortably, and bind this first with the gauze bandage (Fig 5.24) then the ribbon. Fix the ribbon at the start and finish with a glue gun (Fig 5.25). Make a ribbon bow, binding the centre with fine wire, and using this wire, pin it firmly to the foam ball at the top of the handle and fix with a little glue (Fig 5.26).

Before assembling the bouquet, fix 19-gauge wires to all the flower heads and wrap the wires with green floral tape. Push wires into the hollow larkspur and hyacinth stems and bind the wires where they show. The sprays of bird cherry and lilac should have wire stems formed as demonstrated in the wiring section (see 'Arranging Preserved Material', page 50). The foliage will only need to be wired if it has very thick stems which take up too much space in the foam. (It looks more natural if wires used for foliage are wrapped with brown tape.)

Fig 5.23 Attaching cotton wool to the handle of the moss-covered ball

Fig 5.24 Binding the handle with gauze

Make the outline shape of the bouquet using the dried foliage of your choice (Fig 5.27). Sweet gum is generally the best as it has such graceful curves. In much the same way as you would make an arrangement, use greenery to fill out the entire shape, but do not overdo it and make it too thick at this stage. For added security take out each piece and dip the end into a good strong PVA glue then replace it in the foam once you are happy with its position.

Fig 5.25 Using a glue gun to fix a ribbon to the handle

Fig 5.27 Use foliage of your choice to create a long graceful outline

Fig 5.26 Fixing a ribbon to the top of the handle

Fig 5.28 Adding flowers to the bouquet

Fig 5.29 Gluing the lower flowers in place

When there is enough foliage in place, start adding the flowers (Fig 5.28). If the shape is long and trailing it is sometimes preferable to fix the lower flowers to the foliage with a little hot glue (Fig 5.29), rather than have too many dangling wires, which may show. Once all the flowers are in place, poke in more pieces of foliage as necessary and ensure that the back of the bouquet is neat and tidy and the moss ball is well covered (Fig 5.30).

Fig 5.30 Filling in gaps as necessary to finish the arrangement

Wedding Headband

These projects may seem daunting to an amateur, but once the wiring techniques have been mastered, they are surprisingly easy to do.

Method

Floral headbands are usually made as either a half or a full circle. A full circle headband is made by joining two or three lengths of 19- or 20-gauge florists' wire together by binding with tape (Fig 5.31). To ascertain the correct length it is easiest to first measure around the head with a piece of string and use this as a guide, not forgetting to leave an extra 4cm (1½in) for joining the two ends together. Start by fixing ready-wrapped or millinery wires to the larger flowers using the 'U' method described in the section on wiring (see 'Arranging Preserved Material', page 50). Then use your chosen flowers to make little bunches (Fig 5.32) as described on page 51. Once you have enough of these to cover the whole length of your 'U' shape, use a very fine reel wire to attach them (Fig 5.33), covering the wire with tape as you go along (Fig 5.34). Wire the two ends firmly together and cover this join with tape or green millinery wire (Fig 5.35).

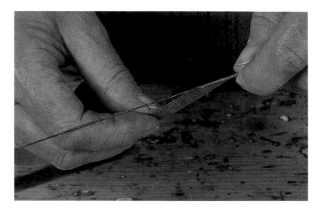

Fig 5.31 Taping wires together to form a base

MATERIALS AND EQUIPMENT

Glue gun

14.5cm (2in) lengths 22-gauge wire wrapped with floral tape (or millinery wire)

19-gauge wires as required

Green floral tape

Fine reel wire

14 *Helichrysum* or similar flowers

Approximately 70 small sprigs of larkspur, including buds

Approximately 28 sprigs of gypsophila

Fig 5.32 Making small bunches with the flowers

Fig 5.33 Wiring the bunches to the base

Fig 5.34 Covering the wire with tape

A half-circle or Alice-band type of headband is
made in almost the same way (Fig 5.36). Start
by making the wire base in a horseshoe shape
and cover it with floral tape, then form a small
loop at each end, which can be used to attach
it to the hair without damaging the flowers.
Make enough little bunches to cover the base,
and wire them in place as already described.
Once you reach the centre, change the
direction of the bunches so that both sides
point downwards at the ends. If there is a small
gap in the centre, make another bunch just
large enough to fill it and fix it in place with a
glue gun.

Fig 5.35 Using tape to join the ends

Fig 5.36 A half-circle headband is made using similar
techniques

Teddy Bear
WALL HANGING

A charming decoration for a child's bedroom wall can be made with strawflower heads glued to card that has been cut into shapes of animals, birds or toys.

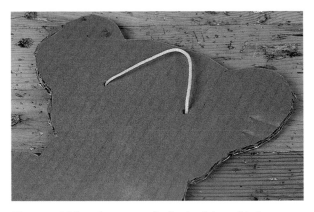

Fig 5.37 Make a hanger on the back of the teddy bear

Fig 5.38 Attaching the bear's tummy and nose with a glue gun

Materials and equipment

Piece of thick card approximately

60 x 40cm (23½ x 16½in)

Craft knife

Glue gun

30cm (12in) length of string or cord

Block of grey florists' foam

Yellow strawflower (*Helichrysum brachteatum*) heads (approximately 3–4 large bunches should provide enough)

7 or 8 red or orange *Helichrysum* heads

3 dried *Rudbeckia* flower centres

Fig 5.39
Gluing
Helichrysum on
to the bear

Fig 5.40
Adding
Rudbeckia
centres as the
eyes and nose

Method

Start by cutting a teddy bear shape from the card (using the template or your own design if preferred), then make two holes as indicated, thread the cord through these and tie it in a knot (Fig 5.37). Cut two pieces of foam, one approximately 15 x 11 x 3cm (6 x 4.5 x 1in) thick for the tummy, and another smaller piece for the nose, roughly 5 x 4cm (2 x 1½in). Fix them in place with a glue gun and carve them into slightly rounded shapes (Fig 5.38).

Beginning with the 'bow', glue strawflower heads to the bear shape until it is entirely covered (Fig 5.39). Finally, attach two small *Rudbeckia* centres as the bear's eyes and a larger one for the nose (Fig 5.40).

Photocopiable teddy bear template to be enlarged to
desired size

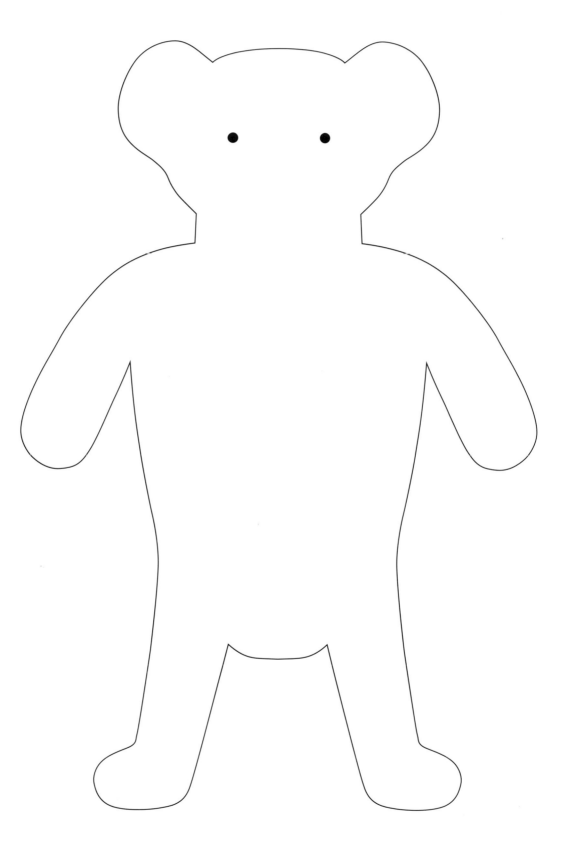

Wheatsheaf
Wall Hanging

OR FIRESCREEN

A flat-backed wheatsheaf makes an unusual wall decoration and can also be used to cover a fireplace during summer.

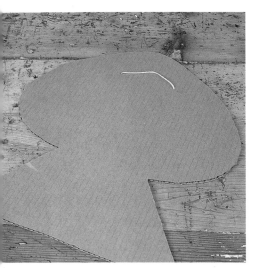

Fig 5.41 Attach a hanger to the wheatsheaf shape

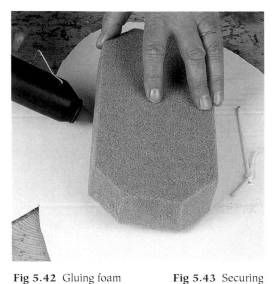

Fig 5.42 Gluing foam to the centre of the wheatsheaf

Fig 5.43 Securing bundles of wheat stems with glue

Method

Cut a wheatsheaf shape from the card (following the template if preferred) and make two holes to thread the string or cord through, then tie this in a knot (Fig 5.41). Cut a piece of foam from the block, approximately 4cm (1½in) thick, then cut off the corners. Using the glue gun, stick this roughly in the centre of the top section of the wheatsheaf shape (Fig 5.42). Next cut the wheat ears off three or four of the bunches, but do not dispose of the stems.

Start by cleaning the ragged pieces off the stems, then using twine to tie the tops, make seven little bundles from the cleaned wheat stems, each one approximately 3cm (1in) in diameter. Glue these to the base to form the stem of the sheaf and spread plenty of hot glue around the tops of the bundles to hold them firmly in place (Fig 5.43). Finish this by gluing individual stems over the tops of the bundles in order to cover the twine (Fig 5.44).

Fig 5.44 Covering the twine with individual stems

MATERIALS AND EQUIPMENT

Piece of thick card approximately 45 x 45cm

(17½ x 17½in)

Craft knife

Glue gun

30cm (12in) length of string or cord

Block of grey florists' foam

Approximately 5 large bunches of wheat

19-gauge florists' wires

Strong twine

Glue gun

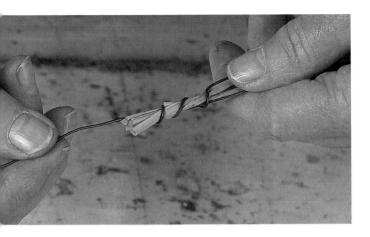

Fig 5.45 Wiring together small bunches of wheat ears

Wire the wheat ears into small bunches, using five ears in each bunch (Fig 5.45). Try to keep the smaller ears separate from the large ones as it is easier to use these in the centre of the sheaf.

Once all the bunches are made, start fixing them in place by pushing the wires into the foam, so that they form a natural-looking wheatsheaf (Fig 5.46). If you run out of space for wires in the centre, it can be finished off by fixing the final few wheat ears in place with a glue gun.

Finally, cut the long stems straight at the base, just below the lower edge of the card, and hang the finished wheatsheaf on a wall (Fig 5.47) or display it in an unused fireplace (Fig 5.48).

Fig 5.46 Pushing the wired wheat ear bunches into the foam

Fig 5.48 The arrangement also makes a striking display in a fireplace

Fig 5.47 The wheatsheaf looks attractive on a kitchen wall

Photocopiable wheatsheaf template to be enlarged to
desired size

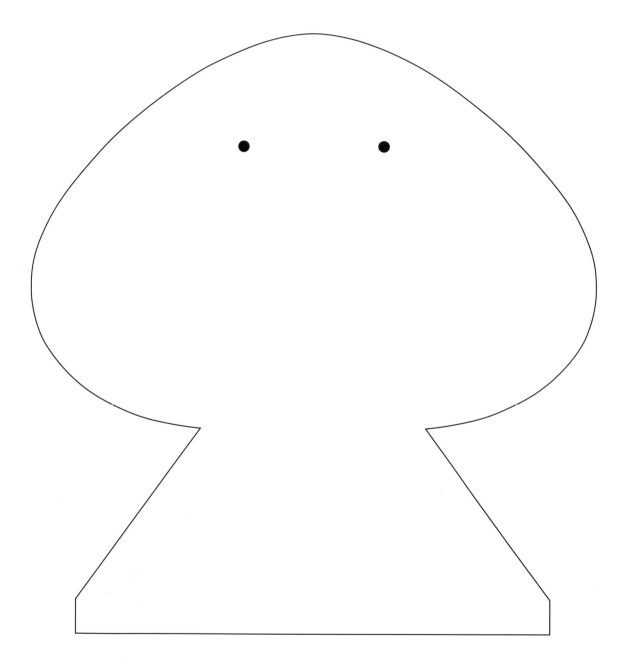

Christmas Table

DECORATION

A festive arrangement made with dried material can be used as a table centre in place of flowers throughout the Christmas season.

Fig 5.49 and Fig 5.50 Attach wire around the fir cones in between the 'plates'

Fig 5.51 Fold a ribbon into a bow shape. Make another slightly smaller bow to place over the top and secure them together with wire

MATERIALS AND EQUIPMENT

Glue gun

Piece of cork or wood approximately 25 x 14cm (10 x 5½in)

Piece of grey 'dry' florists' foam 19 x 5cm (7½ x 2in) wide x 4cm (1½in) high

3 plastic candleholders

Green-dyed *Statice dumosa*

6 large fir cones

6 smaller fir cones

Gold-sprayed larch cones and twigs, sprays of box leaves, linseed, wheat and oats

Green-dyed reindeer moss or natural moss

2 pieces red ribbon 4cm (1½in) wide, 73cm (29in) long and 2 pieces 55cm (21½in) long

19-gauge florists' wires

3 red candles

Fig 5.52 Push three candleholders into the foam

Fig 5.53 Create an outline with green *Statice dumosa* and start adding some gold-sprayed material.

Fig 5.54 Add the fir cones in clusters

Method

Before you begin, attach wires to the fir cones as shown (Figs 5.49 and 5.50). Make two double bows with the ribbon, held together with fine wire in their centres (Fig 5.51). Make some small bunches with the green *Statice dumosa*. Push the candleholders into the centre of the foam, spacing them equally (Fig 5.52).

Build up the outline shape of the display with the bunched dumosa (Fig 5.53), then fill in with single sprigs until you are satisfied with the shape. Push the wired fir cones into place, then the larch cones, box sprays, linseed, wheat and oats. Fill in any gaps with the moss (Fig 5.54). Finally, push the two wired bows firmly into the foam (Fig 5.55), before completing the arrangement with the candles.

Fig 5.55 Add the wired bows to the display

Festive Swag

These decorations are particularly effective
when made as pairs and hung each side of
a fireplace.

Fig 5.56 Iron the ribbon on to the Vilene

Fig 5.57 Make small bunches of green dumosa

MATERIALS AND EQUIPMENT

Glue gun

2 lengths of red ribbon 7cm (2¾in) wide and 75cm (29½in) long

1 length of the same ribbon 77cm (30in) long for the bow

Piece of iron-on Vilene 14cm (5½in) wide and 75cm (29½in) long

Short piece of narrow red ribbon

Small brass ring

Fine florists' wire

Green-dyed *Statice dumosa*

Fir cones

Poppy seed-heads

Chestnuts

Artificial holly berries

Green-dyed reindeer moss or natural moss

Cinnamon sticks tied together in a small bundle with raffia

Alder cones

Method

Iron the two shorter lengths of ribbon side by side on to the Vilene (Fig 5.56). Cut one end into an inverted 'V' shape and leave the other straight. Use the narrow ribbon to fix the brass ring to the centre of the top (straight) edge with a glue gun.

Using short sprigs of green *Statice dumosa*, make 12 little bunches, binding them firmly with the fine wire (Fig 5.57). With a glue gun, attach these bunches in a slightly zigzag pattern down the central join of the ribbons (Fig 5.58). Once they are in place, add the cones, moss, seed-heads, holly berries and cinnamon to the statice (Fig 5.59). Form a large bow and wire the centre, then glue a piece of ribbon over the wire (Fig 5.60). Attach the bow at the top of the swag, under the brass ring (Fig 5.61).

Fig 5.58 Attach the bunches to the ribbons

Fig 5.59 Add the other festive materials

Fig 5.60 Make
a large bow

Fig 5.61 Attach the bow to complete the swag

Christmas Wreath

An outdoor Christmas wreath made entirely with natural materials can be every bit as colourful as those covered in baubles and bows.

Fig 5.62 The wreath base of wound honeysuckle trimmings

Fig 5.63 Wrapping long strands of ivy around the base

Fig 5.64 Pushing sprigs of holly into place around the wreath

Fig 5.65 Adding the sprays of Chinese lanterns

Fig 5.66 Wiring clusters of fir cones firmly into the wreath

MATERIALS AND EQUIPMENT

Honeysuckle prunings

Thick strand of ivy

Holly

7 large fir cones

17 sprays of Chinese lanterns

Method

Start by forming the honeysuckle prunings into a wreath base approximately 38cm (15in) in diameter, wiring it as necessary to keep the pieces in place (Fig 5.62).

Next, wrap the whole wreath with the ivy (Fig 5.63), and push the holly in at intervals around the wreath, always facing the same direction (Fig 5.64). There should be no need to wire it in place if the wreath is fairly tightly woven. Push the Chinese lantern sprays into place (Fig 5.65). Wire the fir cones (as described on page 84) and add them in two clusters of two cones and one of three, wiring them firmly into the wreath (Fig 5.66).

Dried Flower

*L*isted below are flowers and other natural materials which have proved suitable for preserving and the methods which I find most successful. The symbol 〰 denotes that a particular flower will dry best in a warm place such as an airing cupboard. Where this is not specified, any dry airy space will suffice.

Acanthus

Pick the long spires when most of the flowers are open and dry by hanging them in small bunches. They also dry well in the bud stage, and these make a nice contrast to the flowers in large arrangements.

Achillea (Yarrow)

Pick all varieties when each tiny flower on the head is fully open. Bunch and hang in a well-aired place to dry.

Amaranthus

African marigold (*Tagetes erecta*)

The heads dry perfectly in silica gel and the colours last for many years. As the flowers have a high moisture content, they require a longer drying time than most other flowers, sometimes up to 14 days.

Agastache

Pick when the flowers are fully out and hang in bunches.

Allium 〰

Most of the round-headed varieties can be successfully dried once they are fully mature and the seeds have started to set. Some varieties can be dried whilst still in full flower. Stand upright.

Allium siculum
See **Nectaroscordum siculum**

Amaranthus ('Green Thumb' and 'Pygmy Torch') 〰

To retain a good colour, pick the spikes as soon as the first seeds are showing. Hang in bunches.

Ammobium

Pick these white 'daisies' with fairly long stems to ensure that there are plenty of pretty little buds mixed in with the flowers.

Anaphalis

Pick before the flowers are fully out and do not strip off the leaves as they remain attractive. Hang in bunches.

Anemone

The large-flowered open types dry well in silica gel. They take three to seven days.

Artemisia (mugwort and tarragon)

Pick when the flower 'bobbles' cover the stems. Bunch and hang.

Arum lily (*Zantedeschia*)

The flowers can be successfully dried in silica gel.

Aster See Michaelmas daisy

Astilbe 〰

The flowers dry well when they are fully out. Dry by hanging in bunches.

Astrantia ('Hattie's Pincushion') 〰

Pick when the flowers are fully out and hang in bunches.

Atriplex hortensis ('Red Orach') 〰

Wait until the spikes are heavily covered in seeds before picking. Hang in bunches. Though red when picked, they will turn green after drying and last for many years. Drying is not the only use for this plant, the leaves can also be used in salads.

Ballota 〰

Pick when the little flower 'rosettes' are fully formed. Do not strip off the leaves as they dry perfectly. Hang in bunches.

Bamboo

Cut long sprays at any time of year and dry by pressing or lying flat.

Barley (*Hordeum vulgare*) 〰

In common with all cereals, barley is best picked once mature but still green.

Bay (sweet) (*Laurus nobilis*)

Pick sprays of mature leaves during autumn and winter. They can either be treated in glycerine in which case they become a deep olive green, eventually turning brown, or simply dried by laying flat in a warm place.

Camellia

Beech *Fagus sylvatica*

Treat medium-sized sprays in glycerine during September and October. Times vary but they seldom take longer than two weeks to preserve.

Begonia

Dry individual flowers in silica gel for four to seven days.

Bells of Ireland (*Molucella laevis*)

Pick when the 'bells' are well formed and the little flowers in their centres are over. Treat in glycerine for two to three days then hang to dry. This prevents the 'bells' becoming too brittle and dropping off when touched.

Bergenia 〰

Dry complete heads in silica gel for four to seven days or hang in small bunches.

Bird Cherry (*Prunus padus*)

The flower sprays dry well in silica gel and remain a good white.

Bluebell See Hyacinth

Bottle brush (*Callistemon*)

Once the flowers are out, you cannot afford to wait, as they need to be gathered as soon as they reach maturity. Dry in small bunches together with plenty of foliage.

Bougainvillea

When dried in a dark place, the brilliant bracts retain both their colour and shape.

Box (*Buxus*)

Pick mature sprays during winter. Dry lying flat.

Bracken (*Pteridium aquilinum*)

Gather fronds in late autumn, as soon as they turn golden. Dry by pressing.

Briza maxima, media and *minor* 〰

Pick whilst still green and dry standing upright.

Buddleja weyriana 〰

Pick when the flowers are fully out and hang in small bunches.

Bulrush (*Typha*)

Collect in late summer when they are mature but before they go to seed. Spray liberally with hairspray and dry standing upright.

Buttercup (*Ranunculus acris*)

Pick in late spring and hang in bunches.

Camellia

Dry individual flowers in silica gel for four to seven days. Sprays of leaves will preserve successfully in glycerine after flowering is over. They eventually turn a rich brown.

Cardoon (*Cynara cardunculus*) 〰

Pick the heads with about 12in (35cm) of stem as soon as the purple flower tufts are showing. Hang each stem individually.

Carline thistle (*Carlina vulgaris*) 〰

Pick in summer when the flower heads are fully open and hang them to dry individually. Once dry, rub off the brown seeds.

Cardoon

Carnation (*Dianthus*)

The large-flowered types dry best. Pick the heads as soon as they are fully open and dry in silica gel for three to five days. Before using the flowers, it may be necessary to apply a little glue to the base of the petals to keep the shape.

Carthumus tinctorius

Pick whole stems as soon as the first flowers show good colour. In this way a proportion of the flower buds will remain green. Dry by hanging in bunches.

Caryopteris 〰

Dry the green seed-heads by hanging in bunches once flowering is over.

Catmint (*Nepeta*)

Pick when the flowers are a good blue and hang to dry in small bunches.

Ceanothus ('California lilac') 〰

When the flowers are fully out, pick with a little of the green foliage and hang to dry in small bunches.

Celandine

Press by placing the flowers between tissues and weighting gently, or dry in silica gel for about three days.

Celosia 〰

All varieties keep their colour well if dried by hanging in small bunches.

Centaurea macrocephala

Pick the flowers as soon as the yellow tufts appear on their heads and dry by hanging in small bunches.

Chinese lanterns (*Physalis alkekengi*)

Collect when most of the 'lanterns' on the plant are a good red colour and hang the bunches in an airy place.

Chives (*Allium schoenoprasum*) 〰

There are two stages when these can be dried, either when the flowers are fully out and a good pink colour, or they can be left on the plant until the seeds have formed and the heads are pinkish-grey. In both cases they should be dried by hanging in small bunches.

Christmas rose (*Helleborus ranunculaceae*)

The heads dry well in silica gel. Leave for five to seven days.

Cirsium

This plant, being a thistle, needs picking just as soon as the colour of the flowers is showing otherwise they will shatter as they dry.

Clary (*Salvia viridis*) 〰

These are best left as late as possible; pick once the flowers with their brightly coloured bracts cover the stems. Hang in bunches to dry.

Clematis

On the whole the flowers do not dry successfully as most will turn brown, but I have had some success with drying the small blue flowers of *C. macropetala* in silica gel. Any of the fluffy seed-heads can be dried standing upright then sprayed with hairspray before using.

Columbine (*Aquilegia*) 〰

Dry the seed-heads of tall varieties by standing upright once flowering is over.

Chinese lanterns

Conifer

Any varieties can easily be dried lying flat in a warm place. After a while they will turn a very ugly shade of brown, so should not be used in arrangements that are intended to last for a long time.

Copper Beech See **Beech**

Cornflower (*Centaurea*) 〰

Pick the flowers before they are fully out and either hang in small bunches or dry in a very low oven by pushing the stems through a cake cooling rack placed on the oven grid. They will be quite dry in about an hour.

Cornus kousa

The white bracts dry well in silica gel. Leave for about five days.

Cotoneaster multiflorus

Sprays of leaves and berries can be preserved in glycerine during October and November.

Cotton lavender (Santolina chamaecyparissus)

Pick the yellow 'button' heads when they are fully out and hang in bunches. The foliage can be picked at any time and treated similarly.

Curry plant (Helichrysum serotinum)

Pick the yellow flowers when they are fully out, together with some foliage, and dry by hanging in bunches.

Cyclamen

The little garden varieties take three to five days to dry beautifully in silica gel. But due to their fragility, great care must be taken not to crush them with the crystals.

Cynara (globe artichoke)

Pick as soon as the flower head is a good blue colour. Hang individually.

Daffodil

All varieties can be successfully dried in silica gel and take about five to seven days. The short trumpeted ones are the best to use.

Dahlia

Quite one of the best flowers for drying in silica gel. Pick them just as the flowers open or they will disintegrate once dry. Depending upon size, the drying will take about seven to nine days.

Delphinium

A wonderful flower for drying. Pick when fully out and hang individually to start with then stand upright to finish. The colour in the blue varieties lasts for several years.

Echinops

Pick the round heads as soon as they have turned a good blue, but before the little flowers appear. Dry the flowers upright or by hanging them individually.

Eleagnus pungens

Sprays of the leaves can be preserved in glycerine during winter, they will turn an olive green which with time becomes a dull yellow.

To preserve the beautiful variegated effect, small sprays can be dried in silica gel and then wired together before using in arrangements.

Dahlia

Eryngium

The species E. *gigantium* and E. *alpinum* are the best for drying, and should be picked once the heads have turned a steely grey or blue. They can be dried either by standing upright or hanging in small bunches.

Euonymus fortunei

Pick mature sprays during winter and preserve them in glycerine. Remove from the solution as soon as droplets appear on the underside of the leaves.

Euonymus japonicus

These evergreen leaves retain their bright green colour for many months when dried. Simply lay flat in a warm place.

Euphorbia

The bracts of most varieties dry well if gathered when they start to feel papery. Hang in bunches.

Evening primrose (*Oenothera*)

Once flowering is over, the seed-head-covered spikes dry well either by hanging or standing upright in a warm place. They remain a good green and are useful for outlining large arrangements.

Fatsia japonica

These monster leaves preserve really well in glycerine. Pick them when they are mature in autumn and winter and they will remain green for a long while. They also press successfully.

Feverfew (*Tanacetum parthenium*) 〽

The double types are best for drying. Pick sprays of flowers when they are fully out and hang in bunches to dry.

Euphorbia

Ferns (*Dryopteris*)

Most varieties can be successfully pressed. Gather mature fronds in winter and early spring and lay them between newspapers then put a weight on top of the pile.

Fir cones

All types dry easily just piled into baskets or trays and kept in a warm place.

Foxglove (*Digitalis*)

Pick the seed-heads when they are still green and hang in bunches to dry. They will eventually turn brown.

Freesia

Single flowers or sprays dry well in silica gel but the trumpets must first be carefully filled with the crystals in order to maintain their shape. A better method is to simply hang the sprays in small bunches in a warm place. They lose a little shape and size but retain all their colour and it lasts almost indefinitely.

French marigold (*Tagetes patula*) 〽

These cheerful little flowers dry well and retain their colour either in silica gel or hanging in bunches.

Fungi

These can easily be picked off dead wood and dried in a warm place. It is a good idea to first wash them in a mild disinfectant solution to kill off any grubs which could cause them to disintegrate.

Gaillardia puchella

The flower heads dry beautifully in silica gel, taking about five days.

Wild garlic (*Allium ursinum*)

Pick when the flowers are fully out and dry in a warm place by pushing the stems through small-mesh wire netting stretched over a basket or box.

Garrya elliptica

Preserve in glycerine during winter when the tassels are well formed.

Globe amaranth (*Gomphrena*) 〽

Pick the stems when some flowers are fully out and others still in bud. Hang in bunches to dry.

Golden rod (*Solidago*) 〰

This can be picked at the green stage, when it is still in bud or when the flowers are fully out and a good yellow. In both cases it dries very easily hanging in bunches.

Gourds

Either lay them on a dish in a warm room or dry them in silica gel. It will take several weeks for them to dry completely and the silica gel will need to be dried in the oven several times during the process. Whichever method is used, some will eventually become mouldy.

Grape hyacinth (*Muscari*)

The seed-heads can be gathered up once they have dried on the plant, then stored standing in baskets.

Grape vine (*Vitis*)

Any prunings can be used to make wreath bases if they are formed when freshly cut and pliable.

Grasses 〰

My favourite types I have listed individually, but the general rule for any not mentioned, is to cut as soon as the heads emerge then hang the upright sort in bunches, and stand any with dangly heads upright in baskets.

Gypsophila 〰

Pick when as many flowers as possible are out and either hang in bunches or stand upright to dry.

Hare's-tail grass (*Lagurus ovatus*) 〰

Like all grasses, this should be picked as soon as the fluffy heads emerge. Hang or stand upright to dry.

Heather (*Calluna*) 〰

Pick in late summer when it is in full flower. Hang to dry in small bunches.

Hebe

Sprays of the small-leafed varieties can be dried lying flat in a warm place in the same way as box. The leaves also take glycerine well but turn a rather dreary brown colour.

Helipterum

Pick just before the flowers are fully open and hang in bunches. They will continue opening as they dry.

Helleborus foetidus 〰

Pick sprays of the green 'bells' when they are well formed and dry in silica gel or by hanging in bunches.

Helleborus foetidis

Holly (*Ilex*)

Dry holly can be used as a green background to any arrangements. Fresh sprays can also be treated in glycerine during winter. The variegated variety dries particularly well.

Hollyhock (*Alcea*) 〰

The double flowers can be dried in silica gel but as the texture of the petals is very soft, they do not last very well. The sprays of seed-heads can be picked when green and dried by hanging.

Holm oak (*Quercus ilex*)

Sprays of the leaves dry beautifully lying flat in a warm place and retain their colour for a long time.

Honesty (*Lunaria*) 〜

Pick when the seed-heads are green and dry in small bunches or, alternatively, leave on the plant until they are nearly dry and you can rub off the outer layer to reveal the silver seed-heads.

Honeysuckle (*Lonicera*)

Use winter prunings in the same way as kiwi and vine branches to make bases for wreaths.

Hop (*Humulus*) 〜

Pick as soon as the distinctive 'flowers' appear and still have a good green colour. Hang to dry.

Hornbeam (*Carpinus*) 〜

Pick the little green seed pods in June and July and dry lying flat. They retain their colour for a long time.

Hyacinth and bluebell

All types dry easily in silica gel and keep their colour well.

Honesty

Hydrangea 〜

Wait until the colour changes in autumn and the heads have a leathery feel. Using clothes pegs, hang the heads singly on strings or allow them to dry naturally in jars of water.

Iris

The seed pods of any species of iris can be dried by hanging in a warm place. Pick either when the pods are open or closed.

Iris foetidissima

Pick when the pods have opened to reveal the red seeds and hang in small bunches to dry. They will need to be sprayed with a light varnish or hairspray once dry. The leaves also dry well simply by hanging in bunches.

Ivy (*Hedera*)

Long trails can be dried lying flat in a warm place. The leaves tend to become brittle and may drop off, but the single leaves can then either be used in arrangements or re-glued to the original stem as their green colour lasts for years. Alternatively, individual leaves can be pressed and used very effectively around the base of arrangements.

Japanese anemone (*Anemone hypehensis*)

The heads of the flowers dry well in silica gel. The white variety is more attractive than the pink.

Jerusalem sage (*Phlomis fruticosa*)

Pick the green seed-heads as soon as they have formed and dry by hanging in bunches or standing upright. They will turn silver grey.

Kerria japonica 〜

Pick long sprays when the flowers are fully out and hang in bunches to dry.

Kiwi fruit (*Actinidia chinensis*)

The flexible prunings from this vine can be used to great effect in making natural rings as a basis for dried flower wreaths.

Lady's mantle (*Alchemilla mollis*)

Pick when the flowers are fully out but still slightly green. Bunch and hang to dry.

Larkspur 〰〰

Pick the spikes when they are covered in flowers and there are just a few buds at the top. Leave as many lower buds as possible on the plant in order to provide more flowers later on. Hang in small bunches.

Laurel (*Prunus laurocerasus*)

Pick branches and sprays during winter and preserve in glycerine. The process will take several weeks but it is worth the wait as they turn a wonderful mahogany colour and last for many years. Mature leaves can also be pressed individually and they will retain their green colour.

Lavender (*Lavendula*) 〰〰

For both the best colour and scent pick the flowers before they are fully open and either hang them to dry in small bunches or lay on small-mesh wire netting stretched over open boxes.

Leek (*Allium sphaerocephalon*)

Pick when the flowers are mature and the first seeds have formed. Dry standing upright.

Love-in-a-mist

Leycesteria formosa

Sprays of leaves and the pendulous bracts with their berries preserve well in glycerine. Pick in late summer/autumn. They will turn brown in time.

Liatris 〰〰

When fully out, these flowers dry well either by hanging in small bunches or standing upright.

Lichens

Pick pieces from the ground where they have fallen. Sometimes an entire lichen-covered branch will be found. In all cases they can easily be dried just lying in a warm place.

Lilac (*Syringa*) 〰〰

Pick sprays of the flowers in spring when they are fully out. Hang in bunches to dry. All colours will fade eventually to a uniform beige, but they make useful 'fillers' and continue to smell gorgeous for many months. Drying the heads in silica gel is also successful and the colours last reasonably well.

Lilies (*Lilium*)

Most types can be dried fairly easily in silica gel. Due to their delicate nature, once dry they are better used in picture frames than in arrangements.

Lime (*Tilia*)

The seed-heads can be dried lying flat, either on their own branches (strip off the leaves) or individually, in which case they will have to be attached to wires before using in arrangements.

Linseed (*Linum*)

Pick when the bobbly seed-heads are well formed and dry by hanging in bunches.

Lonas inodora

Pick when the flowers are mature and a good yellow. Hang in bunches to dry.

Love-in-a-mist (*Nigella*)

The flowers can be dried by bunching and hanging in a warm place, but they do not retain their colour for long. The best method is to allow the attractive seed-heads to form before picking. Hang in bunches to dry.

Mahonia

Sprays of the leaves preserve very well in glycerine during the winter months. They turn an attractive olive green/brown and last almost indefinitely.

Maize (*Zea mays*)

Leave the cobs on the plant for as long as possible, then simply pull back the outer green covering and lay them in a warm place to dry.

Maple (*Acer*)

The coloured leaves of autumn press beautifully.

Marjoram (*Origanum*)

Pick with long stems when the flowers are fully out. Hang in bunches to dry.

Meadowsweet (*Filipendula ulmaria*)

Gather when the flowers are fully out and hang in bunches to dry.

Mexican orange blossom (*Choisya ternata*)

Sprays of the flowers can be dried in silica gel for five to seven days. The leaves may be treated in glycerine or simply dried lying flat in a warm place.

Michaelmas daisies (*Aster*) 〽

Pick when the flowers are fully out and hang in bunches to dry.

Mimosa (*Acacia dealbata*) 〽

Pick the trusses of yellow flowers when they are well developed and fluffy. Hang in bunches to dry. Mature leaves can be dried lying flat at almost any time of year.

Mistletoe (*Viscum*)

Sprays left over from Christmas dry easily hanging in a warm place. The green colour turns yellow after a while.

Montbretia (*Crocosmia*) 〽

Pick the sprays of flowers when they are fully out and dry by hanging in bunches. The smaller-flowered varieties are more successful than the larger-flowered types such as 'Lucifer'.

Moss

Scrape green moss off stones or collect from under hedges and the banks of ditches. It dries easily piled loosely into boxes and left in a warm place.

Mugwort See *Artemisia*

Myrtle (*Myrtus Communis*)

Sprays of leaves gathered in winter dry easily lying in a warm place.

Narcissus

Dry the heads in silica gel in the same way as daffodils.

Mosses, lichen and driftwood

Nectaroscorum siculum (formerly *Allium siculum*) 〽

The seed-heads can be picked green as long as they are mature, then dried standing upright. Alternatively, they can be left to dry on the plant but should be gathered before they discolour. Either way, they will turn a pale beige colour.

Nepeta See Catmint

Nicandra physalodes

Pick when the pods are well formed and a good green colour. Hang in bunches to dry.

Oak (*Quercus robur*)

Branches from young trees are the best for preserving in glycerine. Pick them in early summer and cut off the growing tips. They will remain a good olive-green colour.

Oats (*Avena fatua*) 〰

Gather as soon as the heads are well formed but before they turn golden.

Old man's beard (*Clematis vitalba*)

Pick sprays of the silky seed-heads together with some leaves and preserve them in glycerine.

Orchid (*Orchis*)

It seems strange that such fleshy flowers can be dried, but any varieties I have tried have been successful in silica gel.

Pampas grass (*Cortaderia*)

In common with all the other grasses, this should be cut as soon as the plumes appear and then dried standing upright.

Peony

Panicum violaceum

This millet grass should be picked when the spikes are well formed and dried by hanging in small bunches.

Pansy (*Viola*)

The flowers dry well in silica gel and last for ages. They can be used in pictures or arrangements.

Pasque flower (*Pulsatilla vulgaris*) 〰

Dry the fluffy seed-heads standing upright. Spray lightly with hairspray before using.

Periwinkle (*Vinca*)

The long trails with their leaves can be dried lying flat in a warm place. The green lasts for a long time.

Peony (*Paeonia*)

Double varieties can be dried easily by hanging in a warm place. By this method they will shrink considerably but keep their shape and colour well. All varieties dry beautifully in silica gel, and far less shrinkage occurs.

Persicaria

Pick all varieties when the flowers are fully out and dry by hanging in bunches.

Phalaris canariensis 〰

Gather these grasses as soon as the heads emerge in order to retain the green colour. Dry standing upright in baskets.

Photinia ('Red Robin') 〰

Sprays of the leaves preserve well in glycerine during winter and turn a lovely reddish brown. The flowers dry easily by hanging in bunches.

Physostegia 〰

Cut the seed-heads when they are still green and dry hanging in bunches.

Pink pokers (*Psylliostachys suworowii*)

Pick when the stems are smothered with pink flowers and hang in bunches to dry.

Pittosporum tenuifolium

Gathered in winter, sprays of this shrub dry well lying flat in a warm place.

Polemonium

Cut the seed-heads whilst still green, after flowering is over. Hang in bunches to dry.

Polygonum See Persicaria

Poppy (Papaver)

Allow the seed pods to develop and mature a little before picking. The best time is when they are just turning from green to grey. If they are left too long they will become discoloured and brown when dry. Hang in bunches in an airy place.

Primrose (Primula vulgaris)

These little flowers dry well in silica gel with a few of their leaves. They keep their colour for a long time which makes them suitable for using to make pictures.

Protea and Banksia

All these exotic flowers will dry easily either by standing upright or hanging.

Poppy

Pyracantha

During autumn and winter sprays of leaves with plenty of berries can be preserved in glycerine. They are usually very successful, turning a darkish brown, and are particularly long lasting.

Rhodanthe

This is one of the easiest to grow and most delightful of all dried flowers. Grow both the pink and white varieties and pick as soon as the first flowers open, together with plenty of buds. They will continue to open as they dry. Hang in bunches.

Rose (Rosa)

Can be dried by hanging singly or in bunches in a warm place, but a much more natural effect is achieved by using silica gel. Single heads will usually dry in five to seven days.

Rosemary (Rosmarinus officinalis)

The leaves can be very effective in small arrangements. The easiest way is to use freshly picked sprigs and let them dry out in the arrangement.

Rudbeckia

All types dry beautifully in silica gel in about five to seven days. Before using them in arrangements, it is a good idea to lay the heads face down on a table and apply a little glue to the back of the petals where they join the centre of the flower, otherwise they easily drop off.

Rumex (Dock and Sorrel)

Collect only the thickly covered seed-heads. Hang in small bunches.

Ruscus

These green leaves dry well lying flat in a warm place. They can also be preserved in glycerine after which they will turn brown.

Sea lavender (Limonium latifolium)

Pick the sprays as soon as the tiny flowers are fully out. Dry by hanging in bunches.

Scabiosa stellata

Pick the round seedheads when they are still green and either hang in bunches or stand upright to dry.

Sedum spectabile

Pick the brown seedheads once the flowers have faded and stand upright to dry.

Setaria viridis 〰

The best type of grass for retaining green colour over a long period. Dry by hanging in small bunches.

Senecio cineraria

The silver leaves can be picked at almost any time of year. They press well and make a nice contrast in arrangements.

Smyrnium olusatrum ('Alexanders') 〰

Pick when the main flowers are fully out and the others on the stem still in bud. Strip off the leaves and dry by hanging in bunches.

Rose

Snowdrop (Galanthus)

The flowers and leaves can be dried in silica gel. Great care must be taken not to crush the delicate flowers.

Solidago See Golden rod

Solomon's seal (Polygonatum) 〰

As soon as the flowers start to fade, dry sprays of the leaves by hanging in bunches.

Sorbus scalaris

The leathery leaves of this tree can be picked up off the ground in autumn and when pressed their glorious red and yellow colours lose none of their brilliance. Being so tough, they are more robust than most other leaves at this time of year.

Sorrel See Rumex

Squirrel tail grass (Hordeum jubatum) 〰

This pretty grass should be gathered as soon as the silky tassels emerge. It retains its colour well when dried by hanging in small bunches.

Stachys byzantina 〰

Before picking the silver spikes, wait until they have just finished flowering. If they are picked too early they become floppy after drying. Both the flower spikes and leaves dry well by hanging in bunches.

Statice dumosa (Goniolimon tataricum)

Pick the sprays as soon as all the flowers are fully out. Hang in bunches to dry. Any that are picked whilst still in bud will not open further during drying. Hang in bunches.

Statice (Limonium)

One of the easiest flowers to dry. Before picking, wait until as many flowers as possible are out on each stem as they will not open any further as they dry. Hang in bunches.

Stock (Matthiola) 〰

The flowers can be dried, but they lose a lot of size and colour in the process. Hang in bunches. (I find them inferior to larkspur.)

Strawflower (*Helichrysum brachteatum*)

Pick the flowers as soon as the first three or four outer petals have opened. Either hang in bunches or gather only the heads and put on to florists' wires. These can then be dried standing in jars or blocks of florists' foam.

Sweet gum (*Eucalyptus*)

Sprays and branches can be gathered throughout the year and dry superbly when laid flat in a warm place. Alternatively, they can be treated in glycerine though they should not be left in the solution for longer than one week.

Strawflower

Tansy (*Tanacetum vulgare*)

Allow the button-like flowers to become as yellow as possible before picking and hanging in bunches to dry.

Tarragon

See *Artemisia*

Teasel (*Dipsacus*)

These spiky monsters are usually left until late summer when they have turned brown. I prefer to pick them in summer when they are green and the spines still soft. They will retain their green colour.

Thrift (*Armeria*)

Once flowering is over, these leave nice round seed-heads, though the dull grey colour is rather uninspiring. Dry standing upright.

Thyme (*Thymus*) 〰

This is a bit small to be of very great use, but both the flowers and foliage dry easily by hanging in bunches.

Tulip (*Tulipa*)

The heads can be dried with care in silica gel. They are not always successful. The variety *T. sprengeri* produces attractive seedheads after flowering. Once these have a 'woody' feel they can be dried standing upright.

Valerian (*Valeriana*) 〰

The flowers can be dried by hanging in bunches.

Viburnum

Most of the round-headed varieties dry well in silica gel.

Virginia creeper (*Parthenocissus*)

The leaves can be pressed at any time, particularly when they take on their autumn colours.

Weigela 〰

Sprays of flowers with their leaves can be dried in silica gel or simply by hanging in bunches.

Wheat (*Tricum*) 〰

Cut when the ears have formed but the heads are still green, and dry by hanging in small bunches.

Xeranthemum

Pick the flowers when they are just open and dry by hanging in bunches. They will open fully as they dry.

Yarrow See *Achillea*

Zinnia

These flowers lose none of their brilliant colours when dried in silica gel. The larger types are best as they make a great impact when used in arrangements.

Acknowledgements

My thanks to Sally-Ann Barrass for her constructive criticism
on reading the first draft of this book.
Also to Sally Phipps Hornby, David and Jeremy for contributing
photographs and to Anthony Bailey for the time and and trouble
he took to produce such beautiful images.
Finally, to Kylie Johnston and Clare Miller for their help
and patience.

About the author

Lindy Bird trained with Constance Spry in fresh flower floristry on leaving school. She later moved to Germany with her husband and children where, in addition to establishing several gardens, she continued to practise flower arranging and study continental methods of flower drying. On her return to England, Lindy and her husband started their own business growing flowers for drying and supplying these as arrangements to private houses, hotels and offices.

In 1985 she began exhibiting her designs and flower-decorated hats at major shows both in England and Europe. She has since won numerous awards including gold and silver gilt medals from the RHS and the 'Grand Prix de Versigny' in France. Over the years Lindy has gained a reputation as a leading dried flower expert and is frequently invited to give talks on the subject and to judge at flower shows. Groups whose interests lie in both growing and drying flowers visit her inspirational garden on a regular basis.

Index

WOODCARVING

Beginning Woodcarving	*GMC Publications*
Carving Architectural Detail in Wood: The Classical Tradition	
	Frederick Wilbur
Carving Birds & Beasts	*GMC Publications*
Carving the Human Figure: Studies in Wood and Stone	*Dick Onians*
Carving Nature: Wildlife Studies in Wood	*Frank Fox-Wilson*
Carving on Turning	*Chris Pye*
Celtic Carved Lovespoons: 30 Patterns	*Sharon Littley & Clive Griffin*
Decorative Woodcarving (New Edition)	*Jeremy Williams*
Elements of Woodcarving	*Chris Pye*
Essential Woodcarving Techniques	*Dick Onians*
Lettercarving in Wood: A Practical Course	*Chris Pye*
Making & Using Working Drawings for Realistic Model Animals	
	Basil F. Fordham
Power Tools for Woodcarving	*David Tippey*
Relief Carving in Wood: A Practical Introduction	*Chris Pye*
Understanding Woodcarving in the Round	*GMC Publications*
Woodcarving: A Foundation Course	*Zoë Gertner*
Woodcarving for Beginners	*GMC Publications*
Woodcarving Tools, Materials & Equipment (New Edition in 2 vols.)	*Chris Pye*

WOODTURNING

Adventures in Woodturning	*David Springett*
Bowl Turning Techniques Masterclass	*Tony Boase*
Chris Child's Projects for Woodturners	*Chris Child*
Colouring Techniques for Woodturners	*Jan Sanders*
Contemporary Turned Wood: New Perspectives in a Rich Tradition	
	Ray Leier, Jan Peters & Kevin Wallace
The Craftsman Woodturner	*Peter Child*
Decorating Turned Wood: The Maker's Eye	*Liz & Michael O'Donnell*
Decorative Techniques for Woodturners	*Hilary Bowen*
Green Woodwork	*Mike Abbott*
Illustrated Woodturning Techniques	*John Hunnex*
Intermediate Woodturning Projects	*GMC Publications*
Keith Rowley's Woodturning Projects	*Keith Rowley*
Making Screw Threads in Wood	*Fred Holder*
Turned Boxes: 50 Designs	*Chris Stott*
Turning Green Wood	*Michael O'Donnell*
Turning Pens and Pencils	*Kip Christensen & Rex Burningham*
Useful Woodturning Projects	*GMC Publications*
Woodturning: Bowls, Platters, Hollow Forms, Vases, Vessels, Bottles, Flasks, Tankards, Plates	*GMC Publications*
Woodturning: A Foundation Course (New Edition)	*Keith Rowley*
Woodturning: A Fresh Approach	*Robert Chapman*
Woodturning: An Individual Approach	*Dave Regester*
Woodturning: A Source Book of Shapes	*John Hunnex*
Woodturning Masterclass	*Tony Boase*
Woodturning Techniques	*GMC Publications*

WOODWORKING

Advanced Scrollsaw Projects	*GMC Publications*
Beginning Picture Marquetry	*Lawrence Threadgold*
Bird Boxes and Feeders for the Garden	*Dave Mackenzie*
Celtic Carved Lovespoons: 30 Patterns	*Sharon Littley & Clive Griffin*
Celtic Woodcraft	*Glenda Bennett*
Complete Woodfinishing (Revised Edition)	*Ian Hosker*
David Charlesworth's Furniture-Making Techniques	*David Charlesworth*
David Charlesworth's Furniture-Making Techniques – Volume 2	
	David Charlesworth
The Encyclopedia of Joint Making	*Terrie Noll*
Furniture-Making Projects for the Wood Craftsman	*GMC Publications*
Furniture-Making Techniques for the Wood Craftsman	*GMC Publications*
Furniture Projects with the Router	*Kevin Ley*
Furniture Restoration (Practical Crafts)	*Kevin Jan Bonner*
Furniture Restoration: A Professional at Work	*John Lloyd*
Furniture Restoration and Repair for Beginners	*Kevin Jan Bonner*
Furniture Restoration Workshop	*Kevin Jan Bonner*
Green Woodwork	*Mike Abbott*
Intarsia: 30 Patterns for the Scrollsaw	*John Everett*
Kevin Ley's Furniture Projects	*Kevin Ley*
Making Chairs and Tables	*GMC Publications*
Making Chairs and Tables – Volume 2	*GMC Publications*
Making Classic English Furniture	*Paul Richardson*
Making Heirloom Boxes	*Peter Lloyd*
Making Screw Threads in Wood	*Fred Holder*
Making Shaker Furniture	*Barry Jackson*
Making Woodwork Aids and Devices	*Robert Wearing*
Mastering the Router	*Ron Fox*
Pine Furniture Projects for the Home	*Dave Mackenzie*
Practical Scrollsaw Patterns	*John Everett*
Router Magic: Jigs, Fixtures and Tricks to Unleash your Router's Full Potential	*Bill Hylton*
Router Tips & Techniques	*Robert Wearing*
Routing: A Workshop Handbook	*Anthony Bailey*
Routing for Beginners	*Anthony Bailey*
Sharpening: The Complete Guide	*Jim Kingshott*
Sharpening Pocket Reference Book	*Jim Kingshott*
Simple Scrollsaw Projects	*GMC Publications*
Space-Saving Furniture Projects	*Dave Mackenzie*
Stickmaking: A Complete Course	*Andrew Jones & Clive George*
Stickmaking Handbook	*Andrew Jones & Clive George*
Storage Projects for the Router	*GMC Publications*
Test Reports: *The Router* and *Furniture & Cabinetmaking*	*GMC Publications*
Veneering: A Complete Course	*Ian Hosker*
Veneering Handbook	*Ian Hosker*
Woodfinishing Handbook (Practical Crafts)	*Ian Hosker*
Woodworking with the Router: Professional Router Techniques any Woodworker can Use	
	Bill Hylton & Fred Matlack

PHOTOGRAPHY

ART TECHNIQUES

VIDEOS

MAGAZINES

WOODTURNING ◆ WOODCARVING ◆ FURNITURE & CABINETMAKING
THE ROUTER ◆ NEW WOODWORKING ◆ THE DOLLS' HOUSE MAGAZINE
OUTDOOR PHOTOGRAPHY ◆ BLACK & WHITE PHOTOGRAPHY
TRAVEL PHOTOGRAPHY
MACHINE KNITTING NEWS ◆ BusinessMatters

The above represents a full list of all titles currently published or scheduled to be published.
All are available direct from the Publishers or through bookshops, newsagents and specialist retailers.
To place an order, or to obtain a complete catalogue, contact:

**GMC Publications,
Castle Place, 166 High Street, Lewes, East Sussex BN7 1XU, United Kingdom
Tel: 01273 488005 Fax: 01273 478606
E-mail: pubs@thegmcgroup.com**

Orders by credit card are accepted

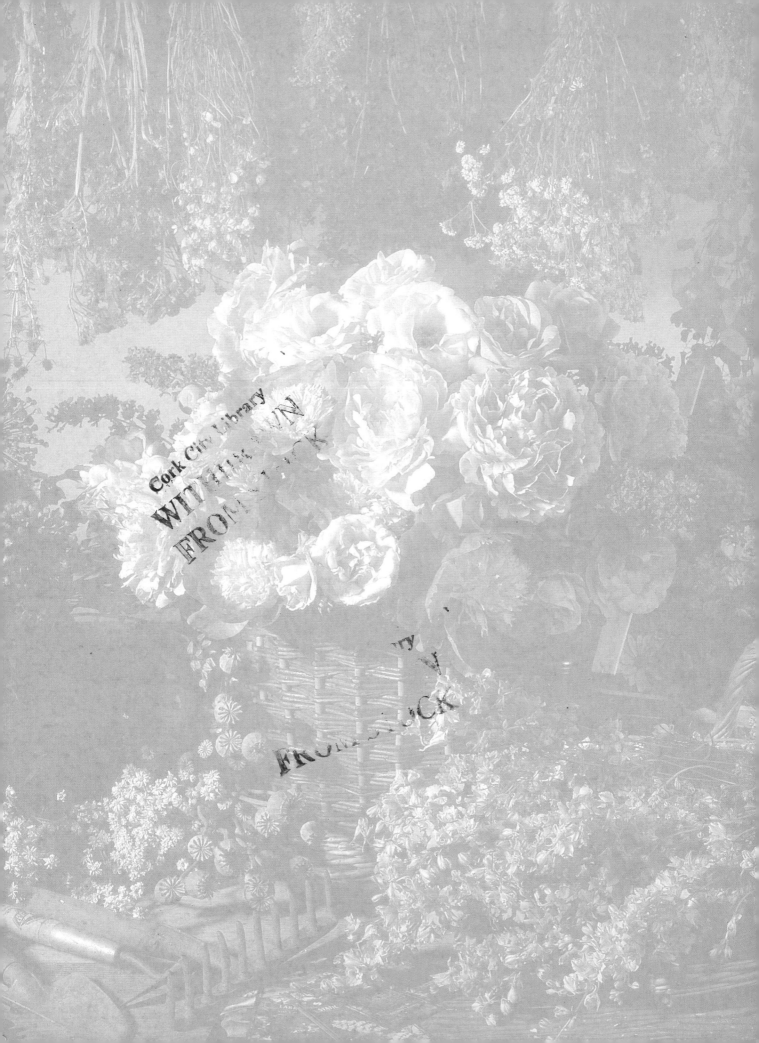